MY GRANDFATHER'S KNOCKING STICKS

My Grandfather's Knocking Sticks

Ojibwe Family Life and Labor on the Reservation

BRENDA J. CHILD

MINNESOTA
HISTORICAL
SOCIETY PRESS

**CLEAN
WATER
LAND &
LEGACY**
AMENDMENT

Portions of chapter 4 were previously published in Brenda J. Child, *Holding Our World Together: Ojibwe Women and the Survival of Community;* in chapter 5 of Albert L. Hurtado, ed., *Reflections on American Indian History: Honoring the Past, Building a Future* (Norman: University of Oklahoma Press, 2008), 114–36; and in the introduction to Frances Densmore, *Strength of the Earth: The Classic Guide to Ojibwe Uses of Native Plants.*

www.mnhspress.org

The Minnesota Historical Society Press is a member of the Association of American University Presses.

Manufactured in the United States of America

10 9 8 7 6 5 4 3 2 1

♾ The paper used in this publication meets the minimum requirements of the American National Standard for Information Sciences—Permanence for Printed Library Materials, ANSI Z39.48–1984.

International Standard Book Number

ISBN: 978-0-87351-924-3 (paper)
ISBN: 978-0-87351-938-0 (ebook)

Library of Congress Cataloging-in-Publication Data available upon request.

This and other Minnesota Historical Society Press books are available from popular e-book vendors.

Contents

In Memory of Florence

MY GRANDFATHER'S KNOCKING STICKS

Introduction

Writing Reservation Histories

In 1900, Ojibwe people performed their day-to-day labor in the midst of a catastrophic dispossession. A half century later, they were still working hard, but they were doing so under circumstances of miserable poverty that differentiated a hardscrabble existence from their former lives of freedom and economic self-sufficiency before reservations. Throughout these fifty years, they unceasingly adapted to protect what they valued most, and what they valued most usually involved labor. This history focuses on Ojibwe people from the Great Lakes, especially the population who lived in the United States during the first half of the twentieth century, and makes every attempt to piece together a narrative of work and unemployment from their vantage point. At times, my focus is more precise and detailed as I write about my own family and community on the Red Lake Reservation in northern Minnesota. The labor history of American Indians who lived on reservations is a complex and dynamic story, one of precarious survival, and must simultaneously take into consideration the multiple economic roles men, women, and their families ingeniously juggled. A huge part of their balancing act involved coping with unemployment.

It is impossible to overemphasize the personal toll of dispossession and reservation poverty on American Indian lives. "Survival" rarely felt like freedom or sovereignty to Indigenous people. The "reservation" was the aftermath of catastrophic dispossession, like a swath of land spared in the wake of a tornado or flood, and the place where Ojibwe labor was reorganized and redefined. The Ojibwe survived the loss of crucial landscapes and valuable resources by practicing traditional economic activities, often within a greatly diminished Indigenous homeland, even as they took part in new income-earning opportunities. Incredibly, dispossession was reinforced by other forms of legal injustice and violence, as when citizens and law enforcement agents within states including Wisconsin and Minnesota openly harassed Ojibwe people and denied them access to income-generating activities over lands ceded in treaties. A vicious trap was set for the Ojibwe, who were treated as trespassers and foreigners on their own homelands, intruders to their own settlements and dwellings. Poorer and less free than they had ever been, Ojibwe people made extraordinarily difficult choices to endure and pursue self-determination. Some of them overturned long-standing gender roles associated with labor, and others allowed traditional forms of work to be reassessed as wage labor. Harvesting wild rice and fishing, along with unusually significant responsibilities such as healing and governing the community, would never be the same.[1]

Exploitation leaves an abysmal legacy, though by appreciating more about the history of labor, we find an essential key to understanding Indian endurance through the decades. My purpose in writing this book has been to explain how the Ojibwe themselves understood and experienced the trauma of American settler colonialism as they struggled to make a living and to thereby shed light on the seemingly permanent inequities we still experience in Indian Country. Dispossessing Indians—and how that interconnects with Indian survival as expressed through work—is a vast and underappreciated story within the modern labor history of rural America. Historians including Brian Hosmer, Colleen O'Neill, Paige Raibmon, and William J. Bauer have established the importance of engaging the post-reservation labor of Indigenous peoples, not only for identifying the countless ways in which the United States and Canada incorporated Indigenous resources for their own development, or the roles of Indian workers in that colonial project, but for a greater appreciation of Indigenous empowerment and resilience. Raibmon was especially innovative in recognizing the breadth of labor by Indigenous people in *Authentic Indians: Episodes of Encounter from the Late-Nineteenth-Century Northwest Coast,* including world's fairs and other public performances, as well as seasonal migrant work, to explain how strategically and creatively they fused tradition with new kinds of labor as they sought to preserve the things they valued most. In a similar vein, William J. Bauer's impressive history, *We Were All Like Migrant Workers Here: Work, Community, and Memory on California's Round Valley Reservation, 1850–1941* relied on the stories and memories from his own people to show the ways community members adjusted their work to a new economy. Despite their many struggles, "labor was both the site and foundation of Indian power, adaptation, and survival."[2]

If we agree that labor was the foundation of Indian strength and reservation survival, how do historians write about it not only with fresh insight but from the perspectives of Indigenous peoples? Many scholars of my generation have believed in and worked to construct the "new Indian history" through our insistence that Indian people are important historical agents who form a critical center in the writing of Indian history, and without them we silence Indigenous voices and privilege the powerful. Historian Jeffrey Ostler has rightly critiqued this approach, warning about the danger of scholarship concerning American Indians that has "deemphasized questions of power, ideology, and the state." In my view, labor history is a perfect site for analyzing the uneven state systems of control and surveillance under which residents of Indian reservations lived in the early twentieth century. I also write history as an Ojibwe scholar, and this book from every angle relates an Ojibwe perspective with my people as historical agents, making it impossible for me to ignore the loss of essential freedoms on reservations during the first half of the twentieth century. As Maori scholar Linda Tuhiwai Smith reminds us, "imperialism frames the indigenous experience" and "colonialism became imperialism's outpost." For me, the reservation of my grandparents' generation was that outpost, and yet Ojibwe men and women engaged in traditional forms of labor in modern ways, found new avenues of support, worked any welfare agency available to them, and appeared to do so as empowered and self-determined people.[3]

Reservation life demanded so much of its residents that even important cultural institutions involving marriage and the family underwent strategic change. This meant adjusting world views. Literary scholar Beth Piatote has suggested that marriage has been overlooked in our analysis of the means by which the U.S. settler state sought to acquire Indian land and assimilate Indigenous subjects, what she refers to as moving "land and individuals out of the tribal-national and into the settler-national domestic." Reservations required that American Indians conform to Anglo-Christian ideas about the roles of husband, wife, and family. To engage up front some of the changes in Ojibwe domestic life, I explored the personal lives and reservation marriage of my own grandparents. Family memories as well as historical documents show that they struggled with all the crises imposed on Indian people during the reservation era—dispossession, poverty, compulsory Christianity and English-language education, boarding school and assimilation, as well as surveillance by local Indian agents. The first two chapters of the book comprise a narrative of my grandparents' marriage and working lives and were an opportunity for me to even more finely sift through and envision the many changes taking place in Ojibwe marriage practices, work roles, and domestic life on reservations.

The book's last three chapters address specific aspects of labor on the reservation through this era. Considering the isolation of some northern Ojibwe communities, it is remarkable how large-scale global events reached into the farthest localities of their society. World War I, the influenza epidemic of 1918, and the Great Depression each emerged as a catalyst for major changes in Ojibwe patterns of culture and work, even as the Ojibwe continued to reside on rural reservations and in the most remote of villages. There is no question that global events had a transformative effect on many of the modern labor practices of American Indians, so that Ojibwe fish and wild rice camps were places where old and new traditions blended together. But even in these work sites and camps, the ways in which Ojibwe people labored or engaged in community life were never excluded from state power or scrutiny, which thus influenced the Ojibwe experience of modernity. Healing, including the performance of dances, was another area of Ojibwe life that underwent change, and like Raibmon in *Authentic Indians* I consider this as a sphere of Indigenous labor. Although poorly understood and sometimes invisible to non-Indians, it was still a site of colonial regulation during the era of assimilation. To meet the struggle of everyday life, innovation in cultural expression, tribal governance, education, language, and jobs and new patterns of geographic mobility consumed the energies of Ojibwe people, but that innovation did not destroy the essence of their culture or their relationships to the landscape of their Great Lakes homeland.

Many of these events and stories take place on the Red Lake Reservation, an Ojibwe homeland with over 800,000 acres of timber, land, and water in northern Minnesota. Even so, American Indian labor across the United States and Canada was subject to the same narrow policies of the reservation era, and the surveillance of domestic life and intimate spaces was as ubiquitous as the Indian agent. Red Lake, Miskwaagamii-zaaga'iganing, one of the largest freshwater lakes in the United States, dominates the landscape. The Ojibwe who lived at Red Lake came to lands north of the Mississippi River after a long Dakota occupation of the region, maintained aboriginal title prior to the establishment of the United States, and along with their hereditary leaders successfully managed communities in the northern part of Minnesota for many generations. Most of the Ojibwe people of the Great Lakes and Mississippi, including those who occupied the small communities on the Red Lake Reservation, historically relied on a diverse economy that included the seasonal rounds of fishing, hunting, making maple sugar, gardening, and harvesting fruits and wild rice. In 1919, after the devastating influenza epidemic, the combined Red Lake communities comprised a total population of slightly over 1,500 tribal members. By the Great Depression, that population had grown to 1,800.[4]

Red Lake maintained both its system of government on the early reservation, based on hereditary chiefs, and its land base, as those chiefs successfully resisted repeated demands for allotment. These leaders unfailingly maintained that the entirety of Upper and Lower Red Lake was theirs. But in the 1890s, without explanation, corrupt U.S. surveyors setting up the new boundaries cut off a large section of the eastern part of Upper Red Lake for the United States, unlocking an entryway to the tribe's pristine water that exists until the present day. This history is not written anywhere within the official story of Minnesota, and tribal narratives carry little weight beyond our communities. Generations of tribal leaders have sought the restoration of the eastern part of Upper Red Lake and the lands surrounding it, and my people will never rest until it is returned. The eastern boundary of the reservation remains a legal focal point today, and has been for decades, as evidenced in an 1896 letter to the U.S. secretary of the interior from his commissioner, M. R. Baldwin, who discussed survey maps and Ojibwe place names for lakes and waterways and stated that "[Red Lake Indians'] occupancy of this country is beyond question or doubt. It would seem therefore, that they are right in their demands and entitled to the valuable agricultural and timber lands (some 200,000 acres) now claimed to belong to the Public Domain and occupied by settlers and lumbermen."[5]

As has been the case for centuries, the fish, game, timber, and plants in the region sustain the people. An Indian agent assigned to Red Lake in the early twentieth century had little regard for the "ugly lot" of "ignorant pagans" at the village of Ponemah, but he still managed to admire "the remarkable resources of their country." Visiting Red Lake in the middle of the summer, he observed the abundance of the Ojibwe seasonal economy at the turn of the century:

> Even at this season they have unlimited supplies of rasp-
> berries, blueberries, and gooseberries, nearly all of them
> have gardens and have raised more vegetables than they
> can possibly use, which they have no means of disposing
> of. There is an immense growth of timber which is useful
> for poles, posts and cord wood and would be readily
> saleable if they had some means of getting it to market.
> The supply of fish and game is practically unlimited,
> the whole peninsula being a famous hunting ground for
> moose and deer. They also get many furs and have a few
> good hay meadows. These resources they keep to them-
> selves and will not permit any white men or any other
> Indians to participate in them, but for lack of market
> they of course utilize a very small fraction of it.

The place described in this passage, Ponemah, is a beautiful small village surrounded by water where my grandmother's parents and ancestors resided. From Obaashiing or the narrows, one can observe both the upper and lower lakes, and the community has always been protective of this special landscape and its resources.[6]

I am an Ojibwe from the Red Lake Reservation in northern Minnesota, one who writes and teaches history, and it has been equally challenging for me to connect and disentangle the story of my own family from the broader narrative of American Indian history. After working as a historian for my adult life, I have come to recognize that my family, like all Indigenous people who lived under the outpost of imperialism, has a seriously appalling story to tell about the most objectionable aspects of the colonial history of the United States. Dispossession, poverty, cultural destruction, paternalism, and racism are the framework of political narratives within American history, but they were experienced by Indian people in deeply human ways that always involved a loss of freedom.

This idea prompted me to write a book—part history, part family memoir—about work, unemployment, and the government surveillance and other hardships of reservations. It occurred to me that although reservations, especially in the past, have automatically been equated with poverty, there has been very little study of Indian unemployment. Moreover, *unemployment* is a frustratingly misleading term when it comes to reservations, since to be without a job that paid wages meant that Indians combined a wide range of seasonal economic activities along with countless hours spent working the welfare systems available to them. Their labor never ceased during periods of unemployment, and few residents had the luxury of a single occupation.[7]

Government bureaucracy placed authority in a handful of federal employees who controlled not only welfare programs for residents but also access to information. Every scrap of communication residents had about welfare programs passed through these agents. In addition, surveillance by agents permeated reservations before the early twentieth century and continued after assimilation ended as a formal policy of the federal government.

In telling a large part of this story, I refract the historian's usual attention away from public figures to focus on the personal lives of my maternal grandparents, Jeanette and Fred Auginash. My family, especially my boarding school–educated and bilingual grandmother, had no choice but to find their way through the red tape of an intrusive organization for the literal "welfare" of the family. By choosing to feature my Ojibwe grandparents—who, as part of an everyday society, lived, worked, raised their family, and suffered periodic deprivation at Red Lake in the first half of the twentieth century—I show this authority over Indian subjects and also continue my research into how Indian people lived with, and resisted, assimilation. I also investigate, in depth, specific aspects of labor—fishing, healing, and gathering wild rice—that express the work of Ojibwe families throughout the Great Lakes region.

How my grandparents managed to earn a living on the Red Lake Reservation throughout three decades from their 1928 marriage until my grandfather's death in 1957 is a complex story that interweaves the Ojibwe seasonal economy with wage labor, various forms of loans, store credit, welfare including Aid to Dependent Children, occasional tribal per capita payments, and a veteran's pension and benefits. For shoes and clothing, they often relied on church handouts and actively engaged in some illicit activities approved by neither the church nor tribal law. Government documents over the years record their "occupations," but to rely on these descriptions alone would be misleading since those records exclude so many of the essential activities that allowed them not only to survive but to raise a large family. Jeanette and Fred walked a fine line always on the edge of poverty, and when illness or complications befell the couple, things quickly grew desperate. Yet somehow, implausibly, together they managed a large household, even adopting and caring for other young relatives or friends who needed their help. Jeanette and Fred were Ojibwe people, and therefore it was their way to take part in labor within a reciprocal network of support with their friends and relatives at Red Lake, White Earth, and Big Sandy Lake. More than welfare, benefits, or charity, this was the foundation of their good life together.

My first book, *Boarding School Seasons: American Indian Families, 1900–1940,* argued for a history of Indian education that showed how deeply families were involved in their children's lives at school. It also demonstrated the rebelliousness of students: in our effort to be sympathetic to Indian people during the boarding school era, we had underestimated them, and sometimes made them appear as victims. As I sifted through student and family letters in the archives, I had my grandmother in mind. She had attended the Flandreau Indian School and was just one of the individual Indian people—students, relatives, members of communities—behind the records. I came to realize that my research was also about my desire to better understand my grandmother and others who endured forced acculturation. That book taught me how deeply assimilation had invaded our homes, families, relationships, and core values.

My Grandfather's Knocking Sticks: Ojibwe Family Life and Labor on the Reservation focuses on an American Indian generation whose members worked and lived through World War I, the Great Depression, and the 1950s. While researching this book, I was stunned to discover that some of my own assumptions about Ojibwe history were faulty, especially how labor was organized long ago, and that practices I considered "tradition" were in fact new approaches to work. This inspired the wild rice section and title of the book, as men including my grandfather were the first generation of Ojibwe to join women in the harvest. Conversely, the evolution to wage labor as fishing became a commercial enterprise involved more continuity in gendered work practices than I had envisioned. The book has allowed me to fill the gaps in my own knowledge about our family, and perhaps similar absences in what my parents and family members older than me realized or remembered about Jeanette and Fred Auginash. There may have been silences around topics too painful to broach. Fred had already survived an Ojibwe removal from the Big Sandy Lake area of Mille Lacs before he married my grandmother in 1928, having migrated north to White Earth and then, finally, to Red Lake. He died there in 1957 and, unfortunately for me, a year and a half before my own birth.

Although I never met Grandpa Auginash, I appreciate that his life has shaped my own and in ways I am still discovering. I often wonder how well we really know our grandparents, though they are only one descent group removed from us, and whether it is possible to shape a credible narrative about the times they survived, so different from our own. Writing Indian history, especially a history in which my own family is represented, is a humbling experience because of all the things I will never know, either through the failure of my own memory and imagination or the lack of a family archive to discover more about how my ancestors experienced their lives.

We are a family of ordinary Ojibwe and working people: no one became rich or famous, we are not from a line of hereditary chiefs, and we have failed in our few attempts at elective office at Red Lake. Other than the occasional meddlesome Indian agents, nobody took time to write about us. As an Ojibwe person, I have always lacked the historical amnesia of Americans, and I credit my parents and grandparents, aunts and uncles, for raising me and my brother and cousins with awareness that the past is how we make sense of the present. As a historian, I have learned enough of American settler colonialism to think through the enormous debt I owe my grandparents and their own mothers and fathers. I am the beneficiary of their survival, and that is why I wish to tell our family's story.

A FAMILY AT WORK

1

Marriage and Work on the Reservation

Fred Auginash or Nahwahjewun of Big Sandy Lake

Nahwahjewun, also known as Fred Auginash, had the fortune and misfortune of being born on Big Sandy Lake in 1888, a decade of crisis for Ojibwe bands in central Minnesota, a year before the state passed the Nelson Allotment Act. Big Sandy Lake is a stunningly picturesque part of Ojibwe Country, today dominated by non-Indians who pay high prices for lakeshore property, though it was once the place my grandfather learned to work the Ojibwe seasonal economy. My grandfather's first decades at Big Sandy Lake must have been filled with turmoil, as the ability of Ojibwe people to control their own movements and ways of making a living by harvesting wild rice and other natural resources and gardening, trapping, fishing, and hunting were abruptly constrained. Through twenty-five years at Big Sandy Lake, my grandfather's future there was never secure.[1]

How my grandfather came to marry, raise a family, and one day die on the Red Lake Reservation, a hundred and fifty miles from Big Sandy Lake, is a narrative of settler colonialism and Indian fortitude, and thus a fundamentally American story. I discovered the most devastating episodes of his biography from the study of Indian history, and some more heartening chapters from our family stories, through which I first met my grandfather.

Just as today, the Auginash family place in Redby, a small village on the reservation where my brother and cousins have homes, is situated next to a shallow tributary river that flows into Red Lake and was the source of clean drinking water in my mother's childhood; she frequently recalled cutting holes in the ice during winter for this purpose. Red Lake people call this spot "across the river." My grandparents for most of their marriage resided in a simple, white, wood frame house with floorboards covered in patterned linoleum purchased in Bemidji, though sometime after Grandpa's death and in my lifetime the house was painted pink. At this time on mid-century Ojibwe reservations, kerosene lamps and wood stoves were the main sources of light and heat. It was a decent reservation house in an era dominated by the less desirable tarpaper dwelling.

Like all families, my relatives are selective genealogists, and as Ojibwe people they tend to cherry-pick and favor the stories that can be exchanged in late-night conversations like comic currency. Of all the family stories about my grandfather, there is one I am able to visualize with no trouble. It was winter in northern Minnesota, a time of year when Ojibwe men found time to socialize in competitions called the Moccasin Game. Grandpa Auginash considered himself a skilled player, and he hosted many of these contests in his own home and visited other Ojibwe men late into the winter's night for this prolonged but lively activity.

The Moccasin Game involves an audience and sets of four players, some of whom sing and drum throughout the games as partners. Four bullets, one of which is marked, are hidden under moccasins. Players use carved wooden counting sticks to keep score and pointing sticks to indicate the moccasin where they believe the marked bullet is hidden. Depending on the audience and their betting, Moccasin Games could grow extremely raucous while the "guessing" and wagering was taking place. On one occasion Jeanette went looking for Fred after he had been gone for several days, taking a broom to Dan Bellanger's house in Copper City, a neighborhood on the reservation, and chasing her husband home. Grandpa Auginash knew many Moccasin Game songs and sometimes wagered to excess. Of course, his fortune occasionally waned, and one time he really "lost his shirt." My mother recalled one snowy morning when she was a girl, Grandpa Auginash briskly walking up the path to the house, coatless and shirtless

My mother, Florence, in the yard of the Auginash house across the river, early 1950s.

after a night of playing and wagering with friends. The picture of Grandpa Auginash striding up a snow-beaten path I have walked so many times, in the frigid winters I also knew having been born at Red Lake in the month of February, is a reminiscence deliberately passed down to me from my mother. She loved the man whom she always referred to as "Papa," thought he was hilarious, and wanted me to know the kind of person he was.[2]

My uncle McKinley Auginash, my mother's older brother, inherited his barrel-chested physique from Grandpa, and also his love of hunting, fishing, and trapping. McKinley's personality and hearty passion for Ojibwe ways of life at Red Lake provided my most direct link to my grandfather. McKinley was also hilarious and a prime storyteller, and he loved to take me hunting with my male cousins, even though I was a girl and he had not only three sons but five daughters of his own. This was probably because I enjoyed his stories, and storytellers need fresh, polite

Fred Auginash,
about 1930.

listeners. Listening to him as we rode the reservation in his mint-green Ford pickup truck, deer hunting at night, were some of the best hours of my youth. He fired shots with an astounding accuracy. Uncle McKinley, or Zonsway, gave me a new Ojibwe name when I was in my teens, after he recovered from a difficult back surgery. A lifelong hunter, he chose a bird he often saw in the winter, Bíne or Partridge, and since we consider naming to be a reciprocal relationship as embodied in the notion of the namesake, or niiyawe'enh, he and I also had a spiritual bond. McKinley spoke Ojibwe and had grown up watching the Moccasin Game and hearing the drumming and singing in all-night sessions. Sometime during the 1970s, he became one of a number of Ojibwe men to begin reviving the game at powwows and other gatherings. Finally, I heard the songs that accompanied the story, and so this memory of Grandpa Auginash's lost shirt has become my own.

Other information about Native grandparents can be gleaned in basic census data and tribal enrollment records, something American Indians have in excess, since the government has been calculating our blood quantum and what band or people we are related to since the nineteenth century. For a longer view of ancestry, we can even pry into early annuity records, from a time when the U.S. government was making scanty payments to the Ojibwe and other tribes in exchange for fantastic land sale deals. According to tribal records, Grandpa Auginash was born on August 15, 1888, to Susan Ahwasegeshigoqua Martin and Jack Nodinishkung Kechegwe Auginash, and was one of two sons; the other was John Aynemahsung Auginash (1887–1933). Grandpa's name appears as Fred Nahwahjewun Badboy Auginash. John Auginash eventually had a large family at White Earth. Fred's relatives at White Earth, where Jack Auginash had an allotment, at some point began spelling their last name Auginaush. My mother and her brothers and sisters were very close to their White Earth cousins. My non-Indian father once told me that Grandpa Auginash, whom my father loved, respected, and apparently communicated with despite a language barrier, attributed his surname to an ancestor Agenose, whose name appears in his family genealogy on the tribal enrollment records.[3]

Grandpa Auginash also considered Sam Yankee, or Ayshpun, to be his brother. Born around 1900, Yankee was a spiritual leader within the Midewiwin, a drum carrier, and he is today remembered as a significant political figure for his work in the 1960s and 1970s as head of the tribal council on the Mille Lacs Reservation. Sam stayed in their place of birth at Big Sandy Lake. When I was a child, my parents and brother and I visited Sam and his wife Ada at their home near Big Sandy Lake in McGregor, Minnesota, and they frequently called on my grandmother at Red Lake. The sight of Sam's feathered bustle and false braids (he was a veteran and had a crew cut) hanging from the rafters of his home in McGregor was not to be missed, and as a serious dancer, Sam was usually present for the big Fourth of July powwow at Red Lake.

Unlike Sam, Fred took an allotment on the White Earth Reservation (as had his father, Jack), but he resided on the Red Lake Reservation after his marriage in 1928. Many Ojibwe never actually occupied the allotments they were assigned, favoring more meaningful places of residence. Some Ojibwe from the Sandy Lake, Rice Lake, and East Lake communities under pressure to remove to White Earth considered taking an allotment, selling it, and then using the proceeds to return home. I do not know if Grandpa Auginash ever resided on his allotment, though he insisted he owned land at White Earth and never chose to put it up for sale.

The background to the Auginash migrations away from Big Sandy Lake and within Minnesota was a political struggle over land and resources, which took the form of extreme racial harassment of Ojibwe and the expulsion of many of our people from the central part of the state. At Big Sandy Lake, Jack Auginash and his two sons must have continued as long as possible to seasonally move and make a living on and off the officially designated Mille Lacs Reservation. No doubt, the Auginash family interacted with new settlers and immigrants who, unlike the earlier generation of traders, resented their presence and way of life. My family was part of a broader Ojibwe community whose members experienced steady, systematic, and sometimes life-threatening harassment as they worked to make a living while local and state law authorities deployed and proclaimed regulatory power over the region.[4]

In the more recent American era in Minnesota beginning in the 1830s, the right of these Indigenous communities to the continued use of their homeland was affirmed in the Treaty of 1837. In early negotiations, Ojibwe and U.S. leaders agreed that Indigenous people had rights to labor on the land being ceded, and so the Ojibwe continued unabated to fish, hunt, harvest, and take responsibility for its resources. However, their treaty rights were contested time and again by a settler society that emerged with the population explosion between 1849 and 1858, the years Minnesota was a territory and the fastest-growing place in the United States. Settlers exploited even the reserved land and resources, openly squatted on Ojibwe land, and deliberately, even contemptuously, planted gardens in plots where the Ojibwe had recently plowed. From a legal standpoint, settlers turned their backs on agreements they should have abided by since treaties with the Ojibwe had been negotiated by the United States. A century of racial conflict ensued.[5]

Ojibwe legal scholar John Borrows has written about the "persistence of Indigenous law," which has often been ignored in troubling ways by U.S. and Canadian courts but is also historically incorporated into the legal formations concerning Indigenous peoples. In recent years, courts have been more willing to recognize the legitimacy of Indigenous perspectives when considering issues related to nineteenth-century treaties. In *Minnesota v. Mille Lacs Band of Chippewa Indians*, the U.S. Supreme Court examined the issues. The Mille Lacs case was noteworthy for the thoroughness of the band's historical, legal, and cultural research, which included the presentation of Ojibwe world views, political ideas, and linguistic understandings in the testimony of experts. Linguist John Nichols testified about how key phrases in the Treaties of 1837 and 1855 related to "hunting, fishing, and gathering and with the relinquishment of right, title, and interest to certain lands" may have been translated into the Ojibwe language by interpreters during the negotiations. Nichols pointed out that the Ojibwe language has fewer words than the English language for "individual ownership of land" and that for some English vocabulary used in treaties there is no direct Ojibwe equivalent. Ojibwe leaders involved in the negotiations frequently employed the phrase wenji-bimaadiziyaang, or "from what or where we get our living, our life," a comprehensive idea often used in prayers which referred to "all the necessities of life," including food, clothing, shelter, and medicine.[6]

Evidence presented in the case uncovered detailed information of a corrupt system in which officials of the federal government and state of Minnesota sabotaged Ojibwe treaty rights and undermined their landownership, as the Ojibwe always maintained. After a century and a half of misrule, I will never forget the spring day when I heard the verdict announced on the radio. A major political moment for tribes and the state, and a victory for treaty rights among all the Lake Superior Bands of Ojibwe, it was also a case with potential national impact for other tribes pursuing similar legal action. Grandpa Auginash and Sam Yankee did not live to hear of the Mille Lacs victory over Minnesota in the opinion: "After an examination of the historical record, we conclude that the Chippewa retain the usufructuary rights guaranteed to them under the 1837 Treaty."[7]

It is important to keep in mind both the aboriginal and U.S. treaty rights held by the Ojibwe while examining the contemptible history that followed. The state of Minnesota seemed determined to fail Indians within its borders. After the U.S. Senate extinguished title to most of the Dakota holdings in southern Minnesota, killing and exiling the Dakota after the 1862 war, state policy and practice neglected to protect Ojibwe lands from settlers. Minnesota Ojibwe people were greater in population than the Dakota and geographically widespread, living in central Minnesota and north to the border of Canada, and from east to west. A series of treaties signed in the 1860s took more land from Ojibwe bands; Red Lake leaders maintained only the center of the band's original lands through treaties of 1863 and 1864. As immigrants continued to pour into Minnesota, a crisis point was reached in the 1880s. It was exacerbated by the work of the lumber companies, which were beginning the task of stripping central and northern Minnesota of its vast and valuable white pine forests. To the horror of Ojibwe families, the dams the companies built to control the movement of logs created havoc with water levels in rivers and lakes, which caused wild rice and cranberry harvests to fail. Ojibwe in central Minnesota retaliated by tearing down the dam across the Rum River, a critical waterway connecting Lake Mille Lacs to the Mississippi River.[8]

The Ojibwe were strong believers in diplomacy, as shown by their frequent delegations to Washington, yet they were continuously stretched to a breaking point. The government showed a consistent inability to recognize the truth of the situation. In 1883 an agent was sent by the commissioner of Indian Affairs to visit Mille Lacs, where he belittled Ojibwe labor practices he witnessed as an explanation for the roots of early reservation poverty, rather than coming to terms with the reality of settler encroachment on Indigenous resources and water: "These Indians, at proper season of the year gather wild-rice, cranberries, blue berries & c. and hunt deer; rabbits and other animals when they can be found, but are often in want because of relying on such resources, instead of making personal effort toward advancement by way of manual labor."[9]

Demand for boundaries between Ojibwe and settler society led to further treaty negotiation and the creation of reservations. These policies culminated in 1889 with the Nelson Act, a politically and church-sanctioned strategy of ethnic cleansing. James McClurken explained the consequences for Ojibwe bands including Sandy Lake: "the Episcopal Church, the State of Minnesota, and the United States agents continued to stress the old theme, repeating that Mille Lacs Ojibwas should move to White Earth." Passed by the U.S. Congress ostensibly for the "relief and civilization" of Ojibwe people, the act emphasized their land and labor. It is one of the most significant legislative acts in Minnesota history, as well as an altogether puzzling piece of legislation. Like the Dawes Act (or General Allotment Act) of 1887, under which reservations across the country were split into allotments, the Nelson Act called for the "complete cession and relinquishment in writing of all their title and interest in and to all the reservations of said [Ojibwe] Indians in the state of Minnesota, except the White Earth and Red Lake Reservations." It was intended to compel assimilation by forcing Ojibwe people to give up their homelands in every area of the state except these two reservations, where they were to take privately owned allotments. All "surplus" land was to be surrendered and entered into the American public domain.[10]

The Nelson Act was simultaneously adamant and inconsistent about Ojibwe removal, as it also allowed Ojibwe people to take allotments on their own reservations. The ultimate goal was to consolidate Ojibwe people on two large reservations, but consolidation was never fully realized. At Mille Lacs, congressional authorization for a railroad line across the reservation and the arrival of more illegal settlers disrupted the allotment process (and also intensified governmental pressure for removal). Red Lake, while refusing allotment entirely, signed the Agreement of 1889, which gave up 2.9 million acres and maintained about 300,000 acres of land and 500,000 acres of water still held in common. The Nelson Act's legacy was Ojibwe dispossession, wild rice habitat decline, clear-cutting, and permanent costs to our water and forests. Ojibwe people had to ride out the permanent storm of this terrible legislation that was constructed to provide enormous bounty for Minnesota's new population and their insatiable timber companies.

During the post-1880s crisis on reservations, the political landscape was so murky the Ojibwe themselves often divided over removal and internal politics. Those who resisted removal in favor of staying in their homes found themselves subject to intimidation and escalating violence from local law authorities. Tensions were volatile in central Minnesota as dozens of new settlers filed entries and built homes on the Ojibwe homelands of the Mille Lacs Reservation in 1889. The outrage continued when Andrew Berg, one of many thieves to settle the reservation, inconceivably laid claim to Mozominee Point, the exact location of Ojibwe summer homes and the Midewiwin Lodge. First the pine timber, then the maple groves where Ojibwe women sugared on and off the reservation were overrun and exploited. I am often astonished by the violence of Minnesota's settler society and their disregard for Ojibwe and Dakota humanity, including an indifference to treaties and other legal agreements negotiated between governments. After studying the Nelson Act since my college days, I am still confounded by the motives of individuals, including Congressman Knute Nelson, the Norwegian immigrant who sponsored the act. And I can only speculate about the anguish within our family that finally compelled Nodinishkung, my great-grandfather, and his sons Aynemahsung and Nahwahjewun to leave their home at Big Sandy Lake for the White Earth Reservation.[11]

What was it like for young men like my grandfather, Nahwahjewun, learning to hunt and fish at the turn of the century, when Ojibwe were often arrested and jailed for these activities? How did he regard American law or justice when Minnesota citizens perpetrated violence against his community, violating their legal and human rights? My grandfather was a boy of thirteen in 1901, when the Mille Lacs County sheriff forced twenty-five Ojibwe families off their lands near Isle, Minnesota, a few dozen miles from Big Sandy Lake, marching them to a public highway while setting their houses on fire. Surely the Auginash family knew about this and other acts of terrorism, violence compounded because it was carried out by men in charge of maintaining peace. Families were faced with the decision to risk future intimidation in their own homes or abandon their homelands for an uncertain future at White Earth. I wonder when the tipping point came for my family. All I really know from records, according to the rolls of 1913, is that Nodinishkung and his son Nahwahjewun had allotment numbers 4829 and 4830 on the White Earth Reservation. Nahwahjewun was just twenty-five. My grandfathers are listed by their Ojibwe names only, and fortunately for my task of locating them among hundreds of individuals with Ojibwe or English names, their allotment numbers were sequential. Jack and Fred Auginash were names they would adopt and need for the reservation.[12]

Jeanette Jones: Carlisle Daughter, Single Mother

Jeanette Jones surely felt that assimilation followed her home from boarding school to the Red Lake Reservation. In the early twentieth century, Indian families on reservations existed under a cloud of surveillance, especially regarding sexuality, marriage, religious belief, ceremonial participation, and labor. The family home was a site of inspection. Working the Ojibwe economy was discouraged—unless it was adjusted in ways so that it could be managed by the nation-state.[13]

All sorts of financial activities also came under the scrutiny and regulation of the U.S. government. Indian agents, school officials, and missionaries were incessant players on reservations, unapologetically interfering in the public and personal lives of American Indians. They sought to control nearly every aspect of Indigenous existence, from how they prayed or danced or worked to what language they spoke. On a diminished land base and without access to many of their traditional resources, my grandparents and other Ojibwe learned to negotiate a miserly reservation system managed by a small number of white men who had access to a large bureaucracy. It was those white men who mediated the bureaucracy and meted out, coin by coin, veterans benefits, wages from family members working in Depression-era government programs or the military, and Aid to Dependent Children and other forms of welfare. They also controlled nearly all access Indian people had to information about those programs. Jeanette learned of this authority early through boarding school, since superintendents there had managed every penny of her meager student funds.

My mother liked to tell the story of how her father came to meet the much younger woman who would become his wife and to put down roots permanently at Red Lake. It began with Jeanette's father, David Jones, who was born in 1886, just two years before Fred himself. One of a handful of Red Lake students to attend Carlisle, David was a strong athlete, and he later played professional football with Jim Thorpe—a point of family pride. Jones returned to the Red Lake Reservation to settle down with Edith Helen Iceman of Ponemah, and on November 17, 1905, my grandmother Jeanette, or Kaybaykezhigoke, was born in her small village. Sadly, Jones would raise Jeanette alone after the death of his young wife five years later. Jones was of the same generation as Fred, and the two men became friends sometime when Fred visited Red Lake in the mid-1920s. Fred Auginash spoke only Ojibwe, and nearly everyone on the large reservation spoke the Ojibwe language in their daily lives.[14]

By this time Jeanette had returned from the government boarding school at Flandreau, South Dakota. My mother always characterized her parents' courtship as old-fashioned in an Ojibwe sense, and as an unlikely romance, since Fred was so much older (and shorter, at 5 foot 4!) and he was Jeanette's father's friend. She was pretty, tall and slender, in addition to being bilingual in English after several years of education.

In Ojibwe communities, it was not unusual for love affairs

The Oorang Indians, a National Football League traveling pro team, October 29, 1922. Jim Thorpe is fifth from left in the back row; David Jones is third from left.

resulting in children to be born of short-term relationships. Both my grandparents had prior relationships, Fred with Chegah-keyaushequ, an older woman at Mille Lacs who died in child-birth, though they had no surviving children, and Jeanette with James Beaulieu of Redlake. He was the father of Amelia, who was a two-year-old toddler at the time of her mother's marriage to my grandfather. But any relationships outside of a Christian marriage were strongly discouraged by missionaries, and people were monitored by government agents on reservations as part of Americanization policies. Along with boarding school education, legal and Christian marriages were required of reserva-tion families and were at all times to be upheld over customary Ojibwe partnerships and kin structures.

Jeanette Jones's first pregnancy was a topic of conversation and innuendo on the Red Lake Reservation. Not by friends or family, who did not consider motherhood in young adult women unusual or "trouble," but rather by the government's intrusive Indian Field Service and school employees. Yet James Beaulieu had a complicated personal history, and so Jeanette's pregnancy was viewed as a potential broader problem for the government employees at Red Lake. On April 2, 1926, five days before Jeanette gave birth to Amelia with her grandmother serving as midwife, the principal of the Cross Lake School in Ponemah wrote to his colleague on the reservation, the school superintendent.

Ponemah, Minn.,
April 2, 1926

Dear Mr. Burns;

I respectfully report that Jeanette Jones whose father lives near Redby Minnesota is at her grandmother's place near Mequom Bay in an advanced state of pregnancy. This girl returned from Flandreau South Dakota Indian School last summer having finished her three year term there and stayed with her father, David Jones, near Redby Minnesota. She got into trouble there, she states with

James Beaulieu of Red Lake Minnesota. Mr. Parkhurst
and I saw this girl February 28, 1926. She said she did not
want to marry James Beaulieu and that she did not want
to go to the hospital for care when confined.

This James Beaulieu was called before the Federal
Court in Fergus Falls Minnesota at the May 1924 term for
some offense against a girl at Red Lake. The other man
in the case of Red Lake I cannot recall his name, got a
sentence and this James Beaulieu was permitted to go.
Now, he is in this affair. This girl has not been here on
this side [of the lake, in Ponemah] for years until after her
pregnancy, then came here for her grandmother's care.
I understand this James Beaulieu has been in other affairs
with Red Lake girls the past summer.

Of course I presume under the law with both the
parties single all that could be done is to make them get
married. In the case of married men getting girls into
trouble something severe should be done.

The mere fact of some Inspecting Official making
a report is getting nowhere. We all locally know what
is going on. No one can convince me the Government
cannot handle the matter and get some results if it is
gone after in the proper manner.

Very truly yours,
Oliver Beekman, Principal.[15]

Jeanette's first pregnancy resulted in the birth of my wonderful aunt Amelia, my mother's oldest sibling and, despite a twelve-
year age gap, the one to whom she was closest. The reservation
school's principal uses the familiar intrusive tone, officious and
meddling, of assimilation policy. His palpable paternalism toward Jeanette, an attractive and sexually active woman, makes
it all the more satisfying for me to gaze into my grandmother's
youthful resolve, finding in her personal agency and a desire
to have control over her own body. She rebuffed the offer of a

government hospital. At twenty-one, Jeanette chose for her first midwife her Ojibwe grandmother. For her three pregnancies to follow, Fred Auginash served as "midwife." In later years she did not choose a home birth, and my mother, Florence, was born in the hospital at Red Lake in 1938. My mother once explained to me that Grandpa Auginash knew how to comfort his wife during labor, had a special technique of lifting her on his shoulder to speed the birth, and grew to be expert at delivering their children.

A month before her twenty-third birthday, Jeanette entered into the kind of legal and Christian marriage demanded on reservations in the early twentieth century, marrying forty-year-old Fred Auginash on October 14, 1928, before the Episcopal priest Julius H. Brown. Perhaps she wished to avoid the kind of scrutiny her first pregnancy provoked. Even so, Ojibwe practices for establishing marital partnerships were taken into considerable account, particularly the ritual of gifts. Family lore says that once Fred observed the tall and lovely Jeanette (my mother said she was "standing by a tree"—it is hard to avoid trees at Red Lake), he entered into negotiations with his friend and fellow widower, David Jones. Apparently he had resources, as he soon offered horses to Jeanette's father, who still used a horse and sleigh for transportation across the frozen lake during the 1920s. My mother, who recorded her interpretation of their courtship and marriage, wrote that Jeanette was "very beautiful, loved to laugh, [with] very soft smooth skin." She reported, "My Father came to visit often and was attracted to my Mom. He asked my Grandfather to marry her. He brought her Dad money, food, canned meat, blankets, a dancing outfit, a load of wood, two horses and chickens."[16]

Their "legal" marriage took place later, in the fall of 1928. I have the weathered copy of their marriage certificate, signed by witnesses including Jeanette's cousin, Mary Jones, and indicating they were married in the village of Redby. Despite the legality of their union before a reverend of an approved denomination, their relationship, labor, and even personal intimacies merited further scrutiny by reservation officials, who continued their interference for decades.

My uncle Richard was born in the summer of 1929. An unusually annoying birth announcement arrived in the reservation superintendent's office later that year from St. Paul, Minnesota. Once again, the topic was "27374-Jeanette Jones," and a letter disclosed that she had given birth to an "illegitimate child." The official wrote, "I am referring to the attention of your agency Jeanette Jones of Redby who gave birth to an illegitimate child, Dick Auginash, on June 14, 1929. The alleged father is Fred Auginash, age 36, of Redby." Six months after the birth of their first son and more than a year after Fred's marriage to Jeanette, he was compelled to produce his marriage license for Superintendent Burns, who wrote back to St. Paul, "the alleged father of Dick Auginash informed me in the office this morning that he had obtained a license at the Clearwater County Court House, Bagley, Minnesota, to wed Jeanette Jones about two years ago, and that Reverend Julius Brown, the Episcopal minister at Redby, Minnesota, had officiated."[17]

But Fred Auginash's word, even an actual certificate of marriage in his possession, was not evidence enough of his son's "legitimacy" or his own legal marriage. Fred Auginash was an Ojibwe man, and even more to his discredit spoke Ojibwemowin. This granted him a dubious reputation and rendered him incompetent over legal issues on the reservation, even the most mundane matters involving his own wife and family. Superintendent Burns would only set the record straight with a reliable, non-Indian witness, the reverend who had conducted the marriage. Burns wrote, "I have not had an opportunity to discuss the matter with Reverend Brown, but will do so at the first opportunity, and request that he make proper return and clear the record in this case." Until then, Fred Auginash was only an "alleged father" and husband.[18]

A Political Refugee within Minnesota

I like to imagine my grandparents' happiness at the beginning of their life together, especially Fred's. He must have been grateful for Jeanette and to find friends, family, and a new home among the Ojibwe at Red Lake, for he was a political refugee within Minnesota, a permanent exile from Big Sandy Lake. Now, Fred had not only a wife and step-daughter Amelia, but a trusted father-in-law, and, at the relatively late age of forty-one, he became a father to Richard, his first son with Jeanette. For the rest of his life, young children would be a constant presence. Even Reverend Brown came through on his behalf, vouching for their marriage.

As a wife and husband married in the church, despite Jeanette's "illegitimate" daughter and Fred's prior wife in the "Indian custom," they now had access to financial resources available to Indians on reservations. Family members recall that our grandparents first resided on Green Lake, the "Copper City" neighborhood in the small village of Redby. Reservation records from the early years of the 1930s indicate a growing family and busy working lives for both Jeanette and Fred, but also a relentless poverty. In the spring of 1929, when $50,000 in tribal reimbursable funds became available on the Red Lake Reservation, Jeanette and Fred were early applicants for a $150 loan to begin construction of a new home. Superintendent Burns, who a year before doubted the validity of their marriage, now commented on their eligibility for the loan program, obviously convinced in the interim that a legal, Christian marriage had indeed taken place. In fact, his recognition of their union now made Jeanette and Fred Auginash desirable applicants, qualifying them for a loan on the reservation:

> Fred Auginash is a Chippewa Indian, enrolled at the
> Cass Lake office. His wife is a member of the Red Lake
> Band. They have made their home, for some years, on the
> reservation. He does woods work a large part of the year.

They seem to be without a home, and desire the loan to
purchase lumber at the sawmill and other building material with which to construct a home on the reservation.
I feel that the chances of repayment are very good; the
home is very much needed; and I recommend the loan be
approved.[19]

Our relatives remember that the Auginash family home I recall, the house across the river where my mother grew up, was
built by Grandpa Fred and Tom Mason in the early 1940s. Jeanette, as a Red Lake band member and the source of her and Fred's
many descendants' citizenship on the Red Lake Reservation,
including my own, would be the partner responsible for secur-
ing a home site. Her husband was not eligible because he was a
member of the Sandy Lake band and had taken an allotment on
the White Earth Reservation. Not until October 1943 was Jeanette's "grant of standard assignment" for a later home issued, described as a tract of land "Lot No 1 in Block 25, Lots 19 and 20 on
the Bank of Mud River in Redby Village on the Red Lake Indian
Reservation."[20]

Red Lake is unique among the Ojibwe lands in the United
States as a unalloted reservation, where land is held in common.
There is a contentious history behind this status. The Nelson
Act of 1889, which demanded that the Ojibwe in Minnesota sign
away and give up "all title and interest in and to all the reservations" in the state, save the White Earth and Red Lake Reservations, led directly to this reality. Red Lake leaders were forced
to drastically reduce the size of their homeland in 1889, yet they
resisted the fast-track to dispossession under the guise of reservation allotment planned by Minnesota politicians, a policy vigorously driven by the United States in the late nineteenth and
early twentieth centuries. Since land was held in common at Red
Lake, Jeanette was "entitled only to the use and occupancy of the
land and tribal improvements thereon" and the land "may not be
sold, but may be changed for another assignment" by approval

of the tribal council. Her assignment also specified that "timber on the lot might be cut, but only for domestic use." Provisions for the future ensured that the assignee was allowed to "designate in writing a person whom he wishes to receive his assignment" after his (or her) death, provided that person was eligible.[21]

Land assignments gave consideration to situations like my grandparents', noting that when "an assignee married to a white spouse or to an Indian spouse not a member of the Red Lake Band, the surviving white or Indian spouse shall not be eligible for reassignment of the land, but shall be entitled to compensation from the new assignee." Jeanette's land proved to be of lasting importance to our family, and after her death in 1987 at age eighty-two, my mother and father built a new house for their retirement there, and my brother, Brian, still resides on the same assignment of land approved by the General Council of the Red Lake Band of Chippewa Indians in 1943. Since then, the Auginash family considers it home, and we frequently gather there across the river in Redby, near the waters of Red Lake.

After reestablishing his life on a new reservation, Fred Auginash was able to benefit from his earlier military service. Grandma Auginash always held onto her husband's U.S. Army discharge papers, keeping them safe in a black trunk; that these faded and yellowed papers are in my possession close to a century later testifies to their genuine value to my family. The first document I can find that lists an occupation for my grandfather is an honorable discharge from the U.S. Army on November 10, 1918, from Camp Lewis, Washington, which also says he was discharged "by reason of not possessing the required degree of adaptability for military service." In that terse language used by the army, there is the briefest description of his appearance as a younger man, simply stating that he was 5 foot 4, dark haired, with dark eyes, and a dark complexion. There is no mention that he is American Indian, though race is certainly implied by his "dark complexion," nor is there an actual physical disqualification. The paper affirms that he was born in Sandy Lake in the state of Minnesota, enlisted in the army when he was thirty years old, and was "by occupation a logger." A copy of his papers certified in 1919 in Mahnomen County, Minnesota, suggests that he was either visiting his father at White Earth or residing there himself after his discharge. Fred misspelled his surname on the document, a mistake not so unusual for a person who communicated in Ojibwe and did not read or write English. This caused some confusion down the road, and as late as 1938 his official correspondence with the Veterans Administration still addressed him as Fred "Aginash." Regardless of the success or failure of Grandpa Auginash's brief military career, it served his family well, since his subsequent military pension was a reliable income in the hard years to come.[22]

The capacity of Ojibwe people for hunting, fishing, gardening, and gathering wild rice afforded them some stability during the Great Depression, even with widespread unemployment. Red Lake was fortunate to not undergo the same degree of dispossession as tribal nations whose reservations were allotted in the United States, making the Ojibwe seasonal round, so difficult elsewhere, still viable for them. In this decade of universal hardship, the Auginash home in Redby filled with children. Richard was joined by a brother, my beloved uncle McKinley, on October 5, 1930. They would be the generation to later serve in the military during the Korean War. There were a number of daughters, including Mary Jane, born on July 24, 1933, who would die after just two and a half years. Some of us remember Grandma Auginash speaking of her sorrow at the loss of Mary Jane, a story which her grandchildren found simultaneously a saga of olden days and touchingly beautiful. My aunt Anna was born September 6, 1935, and my mother, Florence, was the last surviving child, born on August 24, 1938; her birth certificate indicated her mother was thirty-one and her father was forty-seven. Two other daughters born in the early 1940s did not survive long; their deaths were to play a role in a period of darkness my grandmother experienced. The narrow lines of my mother's birth certificate lack the space it would require to adequately explain the multiple roles that balanced out my grandparents' busy working lives in 1938, though Fred's occupation is simply listed as "laborer" to Jeanette's "housewife."[23]

The apparatus of jobs, welfare, housing, and all kinds of financial arrangements and loans that flowed through the hands of federal employees multiplied during the Great Depression. To survive this and other decades of their marriage, my grandparents needed far more than just a desire to work hard. They needed ingenuity and the skills to benefit from a paternalistic bureaucracy. In their partnership, the family financial crusader was Jeanette, a relentless advocate on behalf of her children, grandchildren, husband, and extended relatives in countless letters to local and federal agencies. She spoke her mind in personal appearances at the Indian Agency building and at the tribal council in Redlake. Sometimes she showed up in court. In this role, her boarding school education often saved her. Even a small amount of education gave Indians who spoke English a great advantage within the reservation system, and those schooled enough to write and correspond with government agencies had even more. Fred did not possess the same proficiencies as Jeanette, and therefore exercised less power. The eventual loss of his allotment on the White Earth Reservation was an ultimate symbol of his disadvantage.

A Nation of Fisher Men and Women

Jeanette's "housewife" label speaks to the expectations for female domesticity in American life and conceals the reality of her primary occupation throughout the years of her marriage to Fred, which was commercial fishing. Once it became wage work, women maintained the same access as men to participate in fishing, following the egalitarian practices associated with labor in Ojibwe society. Fishing was, undeniably, synonymous with life to generations of Ojibwe people at Red Lake. Perhaps it was even more so on the reservation, once white farmers settled on the surrounding lands where Ojibwe families had seasonally moved for hunting and gathering before the 1889 boundaries were established.

Red Lake leaders vigorously and unceasingly defended these borders, a large percentage of which were water. In 1918, the tribe adopted a written constitution maintaining their system of hereditary chiefs while carefully confirming their separate political status from the "General Council of the Minnesota Chippewas." Throughout the 1920s, they fended off the federal government as BIA bureaucrats and politicians continued to propose that the reservation be allotted. Leaders were similarly vigilant when it came to protecting Red Lake from the state of Minnesota, each time resorting to whatever convincing argument and legal means possible in their exercise of sovereignty, since the state's citizenry never lost a desire to exploit Ojibwe resources or fish in our lake. The history of dispossession and exploitation on other Ojibwe reservations confirms that fear at Red Lake was well founded and demonstrates the necessity of political independence. Miraculously, consistent leadership and unanimous agreement in the band over what we value above all else, protecting our land and water, paid off, since the big lake's upper and lower bodies remained Ojibwe territory, apart from a small though highly contested eastern area of Upper Red Lake.[24]

During World War I the state of Minnesota entered into an agreement with the federal government and the Red Lake Band of Chippewa to produce fish on the reservation, with an objective of supplying inexpensive food to the public to cope with an era of shortages. Therefore, it is easy to mark the beginning of fishing as wage labor at Red Lake. At the war's end, the operation continued with supervision by Minnesota's Department of Conservation, and the state legislature appropriated funds in 1919 for fisher men and women to be paid in royalties for the fish they harvested. The men and women who worked in the industry formed a cooperative on the reservation in 1929, the Red Lake Fisheries Association, and eventually the buildings and equipment were transferred from the state to the United States and held in trust for the tribe.

There are few institutions of cultural heritage and self-government at Red Lake as profound as fishing, which had been consistently organized and managed by the community for generations. Therefore, it is not surprising that Red Lake people often clashed with Minnesota's Department of Conservation, which, in addition to a poor understanding of Ojibwe fishing, held ambition to extend authority over the natural resources of tribal nations within the state. The department rubbed the Red Lake fisher men and women the wrong way and acted in the interest of Minnesotans and not the tribal nation that was a business partner, but both parties continued in the relationship through the Great Depression. By 1943 when the transfer from the state was complete, the fishery in Redby included a fish hatchery and buildings as well as a warehouse and freezing plant on the south shore of Lower Red Lake, all located a very short distance from the Auginash home. The transfer was initiated in an era when Washington encouraged tribal enterprise. Although heavy-handed management continued throughout the next period of the fishery's history, the federal government embraced more fair dealings for Indians than the Department of Conservation had earlier allowed.

The Red Lake Fisheries Association, formed in 1929, exists until the present day, and the Auginash family continues to have members. The first of our family's direct ancestors to belong were Jeanette Auginash and her father, David Jones. Minutes of the association's annual meetings dating from the 1920s through the following decades indicate a wide range of active and productive members from across the reservation, many of whom were women. While records are unfortunately incomplete for some years during the Great Depression, the name Jeanette Auginash appears on the long roll call of members attending the annual meeting in 1937, 1938, and 1939. Since the list was alphabetic, hers is also the first name on the roll. Jeanette's father, David Jones, would pass away from cancer in 1939, but later McKinley, her second son, also begins to appear in fisheries records. In the roll call taken in 1956, 1957, and 1958, Jeanette and McKinley both appear as association members, though McKinley had likely been a member earlier following his return to Red Lake after military service. At the peak of membership, about 240 Red Lake Ojibwe were working and voting members of the association. At the same time, this number does not accurately attest to the population of Ojibwe families at Red Lake who benefitted from a member's income, because the labor of fishing was shared by so many relatives. The income paid to two hundred members likely benefitted a "thousand members of the band," according to one important tribal official.[25]

Even after commercial fishing and the establishment of the Red Lake Fisheries Association, fishing continued to be a joint family project. The métier of fishing required a number of fast and synchronized hands available to set, repair, and hang nets and retrieve them from the lake by boat. Fish camps were dynamic, multigenerational work sites on the reservation. Fishing men and women, and often their relatives both young and old, bustled at their work, quickly pulling the fish one by one from gill nets before the day's haul was transferred to fish boxes full of crushed ice and delivered fresh into the fishery for weighing and processing.

Fred was also a fisherman as a working member of a family collective. While his marriage to Jeanette afforded him some hunting and fishing privileges on the reservation, he was not eligible for membership in the Red Lake Fisheries Association. My older relatives remember the location of our great-grandfather David Jones's fish camp by the lake, though the Auginash family home in Redby was also a work site, one conveniently located right across the road from the fishery. The eldest cousin of my generation, Richard's son Gerald, was born in 1948 and adopted and raised by Fred and Jeanette, and he recalled the fish camps of his childhood in the 1950s, an era when Fred was often sick and his younger wife's fishing labor was critical to the family's livelihood. Gerald pointed out that Grandma Auginash would "bring a few nets to set, often working with McKinley and David Jones. Ten nets was a lot in those days. Grandma fished, not Grandpa. It was a family thing. Many people helped out from across the river." A dozen nets might yield as many as three to four hundred walleye. Indeed, fishing was a way of life in every village on the Red Lake Reservation, where over two hundred men and women, including spiritual leaders, housewives, hereditary chiefs, and officers of the tribal council, had nets hanging in their yard and were members of the association.[26]

The Red Lake Reservation, for all its diversity of lakes, peat bogs, forests, and productive farmland in the west, was not a region noted for wild rice production. It was necessary for the Auginash family to meet up with Fred's White Earth father and relatives for wild rice harvesting at locations including the superb shallow waters of Rice Lake in Clearwater County. Keeping in mind that Ojibwe people had for generations harvested wild rice at Rice Lake, with our band's recurring land cessions in 1863 and 1864, 1889, and 1902, some of the best places for harvesting wild rice by my grandparents' time existed beyond the reservation's borders. In the traditional Ojibwe wild rice harvest, labor was performed by large collectives of women, and Jeanette's most frequent ricing partner was her friend Nina King. Men often helped set up rice camps and hunted waterfowl during the wild rice season. It appears these patterns would hold fast until the Great Depression. My mother, Florence, remembered the fish, wild rice, and maple sugar camps during her childhood in the 1940s, a period which often involved absences by her parents when they needed to travel to work sites for the wild rice harvest. As the youngest child in the family, she naturally had mixed feelings about the occasions when her mother and father departed from home, knowing she might not see them again for several weeks. At these times her oldest siblings were left as caretakers.

Together, Fred and Jeanette also harvested great quantities of maple syrup, and their grandson Gerald remembered that, though neither of them ever drove or owned a car, "they were the last few people when I was growing up who had a sugar camp right in front of the house, the maple trees were full of cans, and in front of the fishery. We hauled the cans back to the house by pulling a small wagon, and they processed maple sugar in front of their house." While Jeanette and Fred also had a line of credit and shopped at Stayberg's Store and other grocers in Redby, purchasing Malt-O-Meal, white flour, and tea, for the most part they maintained their household through a steady diet of traditional Ojibwe foods. My mother liked to tell stories of times as a young girl she went shopping with her father at Stayberg's, and how he delighted in pretending to the non-Indians who owned the grocery store that he knew few words of English. A favorite ploy was to present a verbal shopping list of "mouse-o-meal" and other ridiculous items to the person behind the counter.

Jeanette had a cookstove in her kitchen and was an excellent baker, always making large quantities of sourdough biscuits and cinnamon rolls to be shared around the table with coffee or tea for those who dropped by. Ojibwe people love to laugh and socialize, and there was a daily stream of children and visitors walking the paths to and from the house across the river. It was a pleasant time when very few friends or relatives had cars and everyone conversed in Ojibwe. My mother recalled how Jeanette "loved to bake, have fresh sourdough biscuits, baked beans, and baked white fish" and frequently reminded her children "never be stingy, always feed someone food when they visit," remarking that "her friends never went hungry when they were at her home." Jeanette added a teaspoon of salt when she wanted to use her sourdough starter for biscuits, or mixed it sweeter with a half cup of sugar into "a soft liquid for pancakes." Fred appreciated her sourdough bread and, my mother reported, her knack for "making it just right for my Dad when he came home." A favorite time of day for Red Lake families arrived early, as Jeanette, Fred, Richard, and McKinley "came home from fishing in the mornings." Ojibwe work and diets were in transition, but our family relished the maple syrup and sugar, wild rice and blueberries, moose meat and venison. Then again, the spirit of Red Lake people is often expressed through the shared labor of fishing and our enduring relationship to the extraordinary, freshly caught fish from our lake.[27]

He Mistook Fred Auginash for a Bear

The Auginash family remembers a tragedy involving my grandfather from decades ago when he was accidently shot on the reservation. I never expected to find an account of this event, especially from so many perspectives, including my grandfather's. His shooting in 1934 produced a crisis within the Auginash family and is a story best told through historical documents.[28]

William T. Kroll, Director, Division of Soldiers' Welfare,
2694 University Avenue, St. Paul, Minn., Attention of
Mr. E. C. Butler, Director in Charge, Rural Relief

Red Lake, Minn.,
Nov. 1, 1934

My dear Sir:

Will you please refer to my letter of September 25 and your reply of October 2; also to the formal application of Mrs. Fred Auginash, Redby, Minnesota for relief because of the inability of her husband, Fred Auginash, World War veteran, to support his family because of an accident sustained by him, as explained in the above-mentioned letter.

This family, consisting of husband, wife and three children, are in destitute circumstances. Anything that you can do to hurry along relief of some kind will be very much appreciated. Circumstances justify immediate consideration of this claim.

Will you kindly advise me by letter.

Sincerely,

Harlow E. Burt, Service Officer[29]

JOE BROWN— SHOT FROM HERE
HIS—STATMENT

TOP OF HILL

MEASUREMENTS: BY H.F.BURT. GEO CHASE— GIDER OF LOSSIER. 89-10-34. 1:30 P.M.

ROAD TRACKS— CLEAR
ROAD VISIBILITY— GOOD
SIDES OF ROAD— BRUSHY— SKUMAC ETC.

WHERE AUGUSASH— WAS SHOT
ACCORDING TO BROWN.

WHERE BROWN FIRST SAW OBJECT—
HIS STATMENT

FOOT OF HILL

A sketch map made as part of the investigation of the shooting, 1934.

Statement of Jack Auginash, Rice Lake, Minnesota, father, and Jeanette Auginash, Redby, Minnesota, wife of Fred Auginash, reported to the Agency on Monday morning, September 10, 1934, and requested that an investigation be made by the Agency officials:

Fred Auginash was shot Saturday evening about 6:30 p.m., September 8, 1934, while walking on a woods road south of the Daniel Needham place, on the Red Lake Indian Reservation. The shot was fired by Joe Brown, an Indian, a short distance off the road in the woods. Joe Brown started to run away, Fred called, and he returned and assisted him to Daniel Needham's place. Daniel Needham brought him to the Red Lake Hospital.

Statement of Daniel Needham, a Red Lake Indian, made in the presence of Harlow E. Burt, Senior Clerk, Red Lake Agency, and John Smith, Agency Policeman:

Saturday evening, September 8, about 8:15 or 8:30, it was dark. Joe Brown came to my house and asked if I would take him to the hospital; that he had accidentally shot a man. I said, "Yes." The man shot was Fred Auginash. On our way home from the hospital Joe Brown and I were alone in the car. He stated that he was on his way home; that it was getting dark. He looked around, saw something coming up a hill. He thought it a bear and shot; a man hollered about 100 yards away. He went to him and discovered Fred Auginash.[30]

Statement made by Joe Brown, in the presence of Harlow E. Burt, Senior Clerk, Red Lake Agency; George Chase and Gilbert Lussier, Agency police, at the scene of the accident on Monday, September 10, 1934:

I went deer hunting about 4:00 p.m. Saturday, September 8, in the Chain Lake and lower part of the reservation. I was coming home, walking north on trail road. About 8:00 or after that evening, I stopped at the top of a hill and looked back. I saw an object following me; it was at the foot of the hill. I thought it was a deer or a bear. I watched it until close enough for me to hit, then fired. It was too dark to distinguish what it was. I fired, not knowing at what on account of the darkness, but thought it a bear or deer. I heard a man holler, in the Chippewa language, "You're killing me." I ran to him. He said, "I am going to shoot you." I stopped awhile, then came up to him. He said, "Come on, I ain't hurt so bad." I said, "Friend," in Chippewa, "I mistook you for a deer or bear." I then helped him to Dan Needham's place about 1–1/2 miles away. Dan Needham took us to the hospital.[31]

Statement of Fred Auginash, made at the Red Lake Hospital on September 10, 1934, in the presence of Harlow E. Burt, Senior Clerk, Red Lake Agency, and Joe Graves, [translator,] a Red Lake Indian:

I was walking on a trail road Saturday night, September 8, about 7:30 p.m. It was still light. I could see the road very clear. I was coming up a hill. I saw the flash of a gun about 6 feet away to my front and left. I was walking in the west track. I fell on my knee and then got up again. I was still conscious. I saw a man on top of the hill. I hollered, "You're killing me." He stopped then and hollered, "I didn't shoot you purposely; it was an accident shot." I said, "I believe you are killing me." I did not know it was Joe Brown until he came back and offered assistance. He then helped me to Dan Needham's place.

Joe Brown and I have always been friendly. There is no reason I know of that would make him want to injure me purposely.

Mr. H. R. Bitney, Supt., Red Lake, Minn.

September 8, 1934

Dear Sir:

At 8:30 p.m. September 8th, 1934 Joe Brown of Redby brought a patient, Fred Auginash, to Red Lake Hospital. He was suffering from a gun shot wound. The bullet entered about an inch in front of the lower lobe of the right ear and came out on right side of nose tearing away about half of the nose and some tissue adjacent thereto. The wound penetrates the parotid gland.

The following story was obtained. Joe Brown stated that he was out hunting deer and towards dusk he saw a dark object about a hundred yards away and shot at it. He stated he mistook Fred Auginash for a bear.

Respectfully yours,

A. E. Bostrom, Physician

Geo. B. Sjoselius, Administrator, Executive Council War Veterans Relief Agency, 6-West 5th Street. St. Paul, Minnesota

May 28, 1935

Dear Sir:

Some time last fall I had occasion to assist Fred Auginash, a veteran who accidentally had a part of his face shot off, in filing application for relief with the Soldiers Welfare office and as a result of that application Mr. Auginash has been receiving relief orders up to this time. I am returning your Order No. 1629 herewith with the request that it be made out to another trader (Roy Bailey, Redby, Mrs. S. Fairbanks, Red Lake, Berge's Store, Red Lake) since Durand and Son do not care to fill the order.

In this connection, I should like to suggest that Mr. Auginash be requested to have a physical examination at this time to determine whether or not he is still in need of relief orders. There is plenty of work at this agency now and if his physical condition permits, he should be able to support himself.

Sincerely yours,

Harlow E. Burt

Standing Strong Woman

As Fred mended from the serious hunting accident that took place in early September of 1934, he was incapable of fully engaging in his physically demanding role as a co-provider who chopped and hauled wood, hunted, trapped, fished, and harvested wild rice. The Auginash family went on welfare. I have no way to be certain if it was in relation to this initial sustained period of hardship during the winter of 1934 and 1935, which were also years when the United States moved into a long and sluggish economic recovery during the Great Depression, but at some point Jeanette decided to make and sell beer on the reservation. Jeanette was a hard-working mother, wife, and fisherwoman, and very active in the traditional seasonal economy, but she also dealt in illicit goods, and for many years trafficked in liquor on the reservation.

At the time of the accident, both Fred and Jeanette had fathers who were still vigorous and would have assisted the family during his recuperation, hopeful that he would mend before the busy fishing season commenced in spring. Once summoned from his White Earth home near Rice Lake, Jack Auginash arrived on the reservation in time to visit his son and accompany his daughter-in-law first thing Monday morning, September 10, to the Red Lake Agency, where they requested an official investigation of the Saturday evening shooting. No doubt Jeanette, along with David Jones and Jack Auginash, was very concerned about the family's welfare; Jack would have been especially anxious since his other son, John Aynemahsung, had died the year before. Not only was Fred badly injured, but there were three young children at home to consider and Jeanette had her hands full with the approach of winter. In the north country's coldest and most extreme season, men at Red Lake normally hunted, ice fished, and ran trap lines.

It seems appropriate at this point to explain my grandmother's Ojibwe name, which was Zoongaabawiik, meaning Standing Strong Woman. For the Anishinaabeg, names are sacred and spiritually empowering, a source of sustenance throughout one's lifetime. "She was very strong about situations that would happen in our lives," my mother once explained, her way of telling me what she wanted me to understand above all else about her own mother. Florence fervently believed that her mother's greatest legacy to her was encapsulated in her frequent words, "Sah-gongish, Beshiek!" "Be strong, Florence!" Remarkably, these simple words proved to be a lifelong guide to her and other members of our family. Florence once tenderly wrote, "When I was growing up whenever I was sick I could hear my Mom saying, "Be strong, Beshiek! Even when I had my first baby I was so strong. I never cried when the pain was so bad. When I got you, Bren, she was by my side telling me the pain won't be too long and it wasn't so bad." Florence herself was born four years after Fred's accident, and she would remember an older father, one in his fifties, but always "a good hunter, fisherman, and very strong." In a small village where everyone knew of the shooting, Fred developed a reputation for resilient toughness for surviving his terrible accident, but it must have been Jeanette who urged her husband to be strong in the first few days.[32]

Not surprisingly, there is no record of exactly when Jeanette began operating an informal liquor business from her home, but she may well have added this labor at this time. The trade was modestly rewarding in the days when few people at Red Lake had access to automobiles, which, on the impoverished reservation, was the case for the entire first half of the century.

When my parents married in 1954, my father knew that his mother-in-law sold beer and whiskey. Until 1953 reservations in the United States existed in a state of prohibition, and officials at Red Lake continued to enforce a ban on alcohol until the present day, making for a permanent black market. The sale and use of liquor by American Indians before and after the creation of reservations has a difficult and complex history, and it involves a long list of questionable issues and problems relating to laws, politics, religion, trade, colonialism, stereotypes, poverty, and alcohol abuse, in addition to the fundamental pleasure of drink for many people. When faced with the fact that for years my incredibly decent and loving Grandma Auginash was a reservation bootlegger, the narrative of her working life must be weighed alongside the adversities she endured. As an heir to her endurance, I am thus obliged to measure the choices she made within her world of limited prospects.

Our village clan leader at the time our boundaries were negotiated in 1889, an elderly hereditary chief named Medwega-noonind, was the best-spoken political leader at Red Lake to argue for banning liquor on the reservation. Jeanette's eldest son, Richard, carried his impressive name, He That Is Spoken To. In retrospect, making and selling liquor appears to be one of the most thought-provoking entries on my grandmother's reservation résumé. This lone fact of her extraordinarily versatile work history helps me better understand and respect the prodigious humanity within the multiple actors involved in that illicit trade. Circumstances demanded she be perpetually resourceful in support of a family. Jeanette was an innovative survivor who defied the rules of the federal government, local churches, and the tribal code by embracing the sale of liquor, making it possible for folks to quench their thirst on a dry reservation.

Jeanette remained in the illicit liquor business for decades. Her grandson Gerald recalled that throughout the 1950s she continued to "manufacture home brew" as she recycled and filled "cast off bottles." He remembered her crock, along with the "malt mix sold in Bemidji stores" like the Red Owl grocery where they shopped. Gerald knew it was well established among the reservation community that "Grandma was a bootlegger; this was how she made a living, selling beer, wine and whiskey." She "kept bottles of beer and liquor in a case, in a hole in the floor" which she referred to as the "cellar." While bootlegging had its share of disadvantages, a notable one being a parade of often unruly nighttime visitors, there were also rewards that earned Jeanette small freedoms. In a community where people had great predilection for nicknames, Jeanette came to be affectionately referred to by customers as Shingababokwe, or "Beer Woman."

2

The Welfare of the Family
Practicing Religion on the Reservation

The fact that Jeanette sold forbidden commodities did not preclude either her or Fred from attending local churches on the reservation, and priests and ministers often visited their home. It is nearly impossible to characterize my grandparents' religious views as anything other than hybrid, given the strong influence of Indigenous spiritual traditions in Ojibwe communities and the influx of missionaries well before their own generation at Red Lake. As at all other Indian reservations, Christian missionary proselytism is part of our history, and at Red Lake this meant especially Catholicism. The government boarding school Jeanette attended leaned toward Protestantism, and church attendance was mandated of all students.

Red Lake is an Anishinaabe community with a deep and lasting connection to Indigenous religion, and the Midewiwin continued to have great meaning for people of my grandparents' generation, even for many who called themselves church members. Any analysis of my grandparents' religious ideas is marred by an inexorable demand for Christian conformity on the reservation. Jeanette and Fred were, of course, married by a cleric of the Episcopal Church. They may have chosen this denomination out of convenience, since Reverend Brown had a church in Redby, but also because Jeanette was not Catholic. Fred regularly attended a Catholic church; their grandson Gerald stated, "Grandpa was Catholic, and took me to church with him every Sunday." When Gerald was baptized on April 20, 1948, Fred alone served as his sponsor.[1]

For Jeanette, reservation churches were institutions for charitable giving more so than for worship, allowing her to clothe her children and find castoff dresses for herself. Jeanette knew this charity had strings attached, since it was necessary to profess belief and occasionally attend church services to take part in the end reward, which was not so much salvation but a reservation paradise of used shoes, clothes, and winter coats. Jeanette was a practical Christian, preferring churches that materially advanced the well-being of her family, and Gerald pointed out the modest benefit they derived from her Protestantism, saying, "Grandma was Lutheran, and went to pick up used clothes on Tuesday at the church. I was happy to get the clothes and shoes, some of them were pretty good." On Tuesdays she salvaged the fabrics intended for sewing and for making warm quilts.[2]

My mother recalled Jeanette's Ojibwe spirituality, saying she frequently prayed and always "put tobacco for the great spirits outside under the trees." When it stormed, she covered the windows and mirrors and burned tobacco. Like many Ojibwe women, Jeanette also collected and dispensed medicinal herbs. Her private moments were often spent in the woods, since "she gathered medicine for those who needed it," noting that many visitors to their home were women requiring treatment for "cramps, hives, temperatures, stomach aches" or desiring "good luck charms," and "she was very good" at this vocation. Once a year, Jeanette and Fred visited a local woman with greater expertise, Beshiek Miller, who resided about twenty miles around the other side of Red Lake in my grandmother's home village of Ponemah. When my mother was born in August of 1938, Jeanette and Fred also turned to Beshiek Miller to name their new child, and from then on Florence shared the name Beshiek, Little Calf Woman.[3]

There was a dark period in Jeanette's life during her thirties, when she suffered a succession of heartbreaking tragedies and surely needed medicine, prayer, and healing. During the winter of 1936, their daughter, two-and-a-half-year-old Mary Jane, contracted measles, which was complicated by pneumonia, and she lingered under a doctor's care at the Red Lake Hospital from January 20 through the 25th before passing away in the afternoon. Two days later Jeanette and Fred buried their little girl at Red Lake. A few years later, on May 17, 1939, Jeanette's father passed away of cancer, and her grief, as a daughter who not only lived in close proximity but shared a daily working life with her only parent, was evident for several years. Her father-in-law, Jack Auginash, died later the same year, on July 4 in Clearwater County. Jeanette's misfortune continued when she gave birth to a stillborn daughter on May 25, 1941, and in a loving maternal gesture gave her the name Deloris Jeanette. A final daughter, Dotis Imogene, was born on May 10, 1943, and died less than two months later after contracting pertussis, her illness also complicated by pneumonia. Fred's inconsistent signature appears on her death certificate. On July 19, 1943, the war ration book that had been issued for Dotis was rescinded. These last daughters, including my mother Florence, were born in the Red Lake Hospital.[4]

Tribal Tribulations

There were also troubling signs of financial insecurity. Jeanette supplied a lengthy clothing order to the Beltrami County Welfare Board during the Depression, though in the spring of 1939 her request was turned down due to lack of funds. Adding to her distress over the personal tragedies, by 1940 Jeanette was engaged in a legal dispute with her father's widow, Mary Bush, who lived in Redby but was enrolled at the Consolidated Chippewa Agency at Cass Lake. The disagreement involved not only the house where David Jones's widow resided on the Red Lake Reservation, but whether she had "the right of inheritance to the personal property" of her late husband, which included two other houses as well as horses. Jones's widow was advised by the Minnesota Chippewa Tribe's attorney that even though she lived on the reservation, a judge for the Red Lake Court had decreed that all her husband's property was "vested" in his daughter, Jeanette Auginash. Further, in response to the widow's inquiry as to whether she had "any remedy which can serve to set aside the decree of the Red Lake Tribal Court," the lawyer cited "*Stanley v. Roberts* (1896) 17 Supreme Court 999, 41 L. Ed. 1177," and counseled, "It appears clear that in determination of contract and property rights, that an Indian Tribe, unless congress has invaded that authority, has exclusive rights to control contracts, property rights, and rights relating to descent and distribution. In other words, we start out with the general proposition that where an Indian Tribe, duly recognized as such, has set up a tribunal or a court, that such court has exclusive jurisdiction."[5]

The Red Lake Court firmly aligned with Jeanette in the matter of her father's modest estate, and the judge in the case was the most influential man on the reservation, Peter Graves. Like Jeanette, Graves had left the reservation for schooling, but he returned to take part in drafting Red Lake's first tribal constitution in 1918. Born in 1872, Graves was a bridge between Red Lake's tradition of hereditary chiefs and the modern system of elected council and also lived in Redby, though in a home with a "study crammed with volumes on history, mostly Indian history." In one of the few existing interviews with Graves, he repeatedly discussed what today we would term genocide in American Indian history and "incidents in the history of Indian policy," including "mass extermination" and the government's practice of ignoring Indian treaty rights. While Graves had converted to Christianity as a young man during a period he spent in the East, he tired of the constant stream of missionaries invading the reservation and often told them and other visitors the people of Red Lake "had already given up enough land for God." A visionary leader and intellect, he successfully fought the government's plan still under way in the 1920s to allot Red Lake.[6]

Graves began his Red Lake career early and, in the custom of hereditary chiefs, never retired, managing business and attending meetings of the tribal council until a few weeks before his death at eighty-six. Graves's influence was everywhere at Red Lake. When the 1899 Red Lake delegation went to Washington to discuss land, water, and timber issues, sixteen-year-old Graves traveled along to serve as an interpreter. He worked his way on the reservation from school janitor to chief of police, eventually serving as judge of the Court of Indian Offences from 1936 to 1943. He continuously struggled against the liquor traffic on the reservation. For a time he was director of the fisheries. Formally, he held the title of secretary-treasurer of the tribe from 1920 until his death in 1957, the unofficial "chairman" long before the title existed on the Red Lake Reservation.[7]

Judge Peter Graves wrote to the lawyer for the Minnesota Chippewa Tribe on August 9, 1940, about the dispute between Jeanette and her father's widow, mentioning the lingering acrimony between the two women after David Jones's death and the refusal of each to "live and treat each other the same as they did while David Jones was living, but they would not agree to 'bury the hatchet' between them." Graves pointed out that Mrs. Jones initially accepted the terms of the settlement, saying, "Mrs. Jeanette Auginash claimed her annuity payment money was used by her father in building the home so the division by the court was made accordingly, which both agreed to at the time."

Judge Graves clearly elucidated the legal questions handled by the tribal court in addition to commenting on the drawn-out antipathy between the two women, but there is another compelling facet of his letter, one that sheds light on the complicated issue of religion within my own and other Red Lake families. Graves concluded with mention of the traditional Midewiwin funeral rites held in the spring of 1939 for my great-grandfather, David Jones. Jones was exposed to Christian doctrine during his time at the Carlisle Indian Industrial School. The discourse of Christianity was ubiquitous within Indian boarding schools, and he apparently felt strongly enough about education to send his daughter away to school. At the end of his life, his Midewiwin funeral appears an even stronger statement of the enduring power within the family of Ojibwe religious ideas, more so than "the white man's religion." Graves wrote,

> When David Jones died Mrs. David Jones was in the
> White Earth Hospital. At any rate she was not well
> enough to be present to look after the burial of her
> husband, and David Jones was buried according to the
> tribal custom of the Indians; his immediate possessions
> like guns and personal belongings were gathered and
> disposed of according to Indian custom so I understand
> David Jones wanted to be buried according to Indian
> custom; and certain of his blood relations looked after
> the burial. I know of no law that would prevent Indian
> custom burials on the reservation here as that is done by
> those who have not adopted the white man's religion.[8]

By August 12, 1940, the superintendent of the Red Lake Indian Agency declared closed the matter of the distribution of David Jones's property, and the fact that the "annuity payments of Jeanette Auginash were used in the construction of these houses" settled the matter. The reservation superintendent wrote that he had been present "at the hearing held in Indian Court, and it seemed to me that the distribution was fair, in fact, very fair and equitable." However, the property settlement did not end the enmity between Jeanette and her father's widow. As the superintendent noted, "the whole trouble is due to the fact that these two women do not like each other and continue to quarrel and fight over nothing." The disagreement may have been a legitimate grievance with a difficult woman, or perhaps Jeanette was also to blame, unnecessarily continuing the conflict even after her success in court. Regardless of Jeanette's culpability in the disagreement, her despair was palpable and continued to influence her private and public life in the 1940s.[9]

Red Lake of the 1940s was not only an Indian reservation but an Ojibwe homeland composed of a number of small villages, especially those at Little Rock, Redlake, Redby, and Ponemah. Despite consistent pressure, the reservation was never allotted, and the government had in the previous decade finally abandoned a policy that had robbed Indian people of their land in the United States. Red Lake survived intact, even gaining back some of the ceded lands near the Canadian border. Indeed, it was the largest Ojibwe place in the United States or Canada completely owned by its original people. The population was much smaller than today, with fewer than two thousand people on the reservation. It was a friendly time, when social life revolved around the community and villagers often worked together. In the way of Ojibwe leaders, Peter Graves, driving his black car on rutted reservation roads best suited to horses, often took time to visit residents, especially his Redby neighbors including Jeanette and Fred Auginash. Later, his daughter, Mildred, would marry the oldest Auginash son, Richard. It seems unlikely that Graves, who was known to frequently utter, "All our trouble comes from this liquor," was ignorant of Jeanette's involvement in the illicit trade.[10]

Peter Graves was still a Red Lake judge when Jeanette was found drunk and arrested for disorderly conduct, appearing in the Court of Indian Offences on September 5, 1942. Since Jeanette was neither a heavy drinker nor an alcoholic, a possible interpretation of this episode is that the deeply personal losses in her life had become unbearable. In her mid-thirties, she must have been an anguished person, haunted by the deaths of two daughters and with a melancholy so deep there seemed no end or resolution. Still, she continued to work with Fred. Her older children, Amelia at sixteen and the boys just a few years younger, had reached an age when they would have joined in not only household labor but also fishing activities. It appears that Jeanette's grief temporarily overshadowed the good life she had built with Fred and their young family. On the reservation, binge drinking was a respite, a way to temporarily allow the soul to muddle through the complications of poverty, intrusions by government, and all the misery produced by early death and despair. It is not clear if Judge Graves or a colleague handled her case, since the judge's name is absent from the following court transcript of her hearing.

Judge:

    Q. *What is your name?* **A.** *Jeanette Auginash*

    Q. *Are you a Red Lake Indian?* **A.** *Yes.*

    Q. *How old are you?* **A.** *36.*

    Q. *I have a complaint here signed by Frank Gurno, Chief of Police—about 6:30 p.m. Saturday the above defendant was picked up by police in the village of Redby drunk. Was lodged in jail and was released when sober.*[11]

    Q. *Are you guilty or not guilty?* **A.** *Yes.*

    Q. *Were you drunk?* **A.** *I wasn't very drunk.*

    Q. *Where did you get your liquor from?* **A.** *Some boys gave it to me.*

    Q. *Where did the boys get it from?* **A.** *They got it from town.*

    Q. *Did you buy this beer?* **A.** *No, they gave it to me. I never have any money to buy beer.*

    Q. *Were you very drunk?* **A.** *No, not very.*

Frank Gurneau, Red Lake's chief of police, also made a statement regarding Jeanette's arrest: "She stopped us in copper city and said she wanted us to go and arrest some boys that wouldn't give her beer. We told her to get in the car and she refused to and started calling us all kinds of names. She was so drunk that she could hardly walk."

Jeanette's hearing concluded with a strong reproach from the judge, though Graves or any other person from the tight-knit reservation would have probably known of her recent setbacks. The judge scolded her with the comment, "You were so drunk that you didn't know what you were saying," yet he did not in the end sentence her to jail. To this very public humiliation Jeanette simply replied, "I don't know." And despite his conclusion that "I think you are guilty all right," the judge ended the hearing with only a reprimand. Red Lake's Court of Indian Offences put Jeanette on probation for ninety days, but the judge warned of a future sentence of "jail for 30 days" and admonished her by saying "if you want to go to jail, just get drunk again."[12]

My mother, Florence, was far too young to have been aware of her mother's arrest for disorderly conduct. Throughout her life she expressed deep devotion and respect for both of her parents. She considered hers a warm, good-humored, and unconditionally supportive family and always experienced the greatest comfort in their presence. Binge drinking seemed to permeate nearly every family on the reservation, and Florence acknowledged the apprehension she felt during times as a child when she "would be afraid of my parents drinking beer." Though responsible for only a small part, Jeanette would help spread this plague.[13]

Fred's Welfare Fraud

Jeanette and Fred persevered, working and raising their family throughout the 1940s, always getting by through their established pattern of patching traditional Ojibwe forms of labor like ricing and fishing and other wage work with Fred's military pension and benefits and Jeanette's liquor sales. One difference appeared to be an increasing reliance on the welfare program Aid to Dependent Children. Jeanette, like many reservation residents, also worked several hours a week at the Redby sawmill, earning thirty-two dollars a month, probably at an office job. Redby was the site of a new mill in 1924, though sawmills had operated at Red Lake since the nineteenth century, eventually moving away from teams of sawyers in the woods to a new era of power saws. Land for the mill was leased to the United States for ninety-nine years, and in early decades the majority of workers were, for reasons peculiar to U.S. projects on Indian land, non-Indian. Red Lake's population was entirely Ojibwe, yet jobs continued to bypass the reservation and its people. The work force at the Redby sawmill was indigenized during the 1940s, benefitting the Auginash family, since Fred also found employment there. Once they returned from Korea, Richard and McKinley were also hired at the mill.[14]

On the Red Lake Reservation, a social worker with a small two-person office connected Ojibwe families to the programs available through the Beltrami County Welfare Board, located in Bemidji, approximately thirty miles from the nearest reservation boundary. Caseworkers visited the Auginash home in Redby. On April 1, 1948, the agency superintendent gave a favorable report about the family to the county board, supporting their Aid to Dependent Children application for consideration. He spoke well of Fred's work history, while Jeanette's labor went unmentioned: "Mr. Auginash has a very good work record and the family have been quite conservative in their spending. Instead of putting their money into a car they have bought furnishings for the home to an extent which makes their home quite a bit above average in that respect."[15]

When the Auginash family first began to receive ADC for a short time in 1948, their household included the children Anna and Florence, ages thirteen and ten. After fewer than three months, their ADC was suspended under accusations of welfare fraud. Fred was granted a hearing, and his official statement appears below in English, though it is important to keep in mind that he spoke Ojibwe and this amounted to an interpretation of his ideas. Still, the issue at hand was clearly stated: "Without official board action the Executive Secretary suspended my case on the basis that I had sufficient fishing income. As a matter of fact I am not well enough to fish this year. My wife did a little in June. Her net income was only $15.00 out of a total check of $31.36."[16]

The day of Fred's statement, the social worker for the Beltrami County Welfare Board also wrote him the following letter outlining the reasons for suspending the family's ADC.

Dear Mr. Auginash:

We find that you are doing commercial fishing this year and because of the fishing income, we find it necessary to suspend your assistance grant as of July 1, 1948. If after the fishing season and bonus time are over you find yourself in need of assistance you may apply for reinstatement. Application for such reinstatement should be made before the 10th of the month so the grant, if eligible, can be made effective on the 1st of the following month.

An itemized account of your income and expenditures should be kept during the season and should be available for the social worker when you reapply. Our past experience with commercial fishing shows that the income will be sufficient for your needs and you would be ineligible for aid during the fishing season.

We think that it is commendable that you have availed yourself of the opportunity to become self-supporting even though for a short period of time. We are deeply appreciative of your efforts to earn enough income for your budget needs through the fishing season.[17]

Notes from the Red Lake Agency in 1948 indicate that Fred had been hospitalized at the Cass Lake Indian Hospital for a week, returning home on July 4. Shortly after, Jeanette paid a visit to the agency, concerned about her husband's pending application for disability as a veteran and further clarifying that he was able to do very little work during his illness. She had tried to carry the slack, and records mentioned that "Mrs. A. has been fishing." As Fred's official statement confirmed, Jeanette had received a first check of $31.36 on July 2, of which she gave half to her cousin, who had helped her fish while Fred was sick and hospitalized for "high blood pressure." Further, notes at the agency suggested Fred "will not be able to work for many months—if ever." With the balance of her paycheck, Jeanette had purchased clothing, but still the family owed Stayberg's Store in Redby for groceries. Jeanette and Fred had received a first ADC grant in May for seventy dollars, but the amount was not enough for them to cover what they had already purchased through their line of credit. The Auginash family's debt had risen to $130, and the first ADC check had gone directly to the store. Earlier in the spring of 1948, Jeanette and her children had received grocery, fuel, and clothing money "for relief from tribal funds" totaling $100.80, though once again her husband was ineligible since he was "not a Red Lake enrollee." In September, Jeanette would also benefit from $150 in a tribal per capita payment.[18]

Following Fred's statement explaining his recent inability to work, where he pointed out his wife's paltry fifteen dollars in fishing income, Fred and Jeanette, under threat of prosecution, agreed to pay back the agency for the welfare money they had received from Beltrami County. The document of July 8, 1948, shows Jeanette's flawless signature second after Fred's unsteady handwriting. The statement was witnessed by the social worker: "We, Fred Auginash and Jeanette Auginash, herby agree to reimburse in full the Red Lake Agency for any relief issued on this date or later at such time as Mr. Fred Auginash receives his veteran's disability compensation. We understand that if we do not do so we are liable to prosecution in the Court of Indian Offences."[19]

Later that summer, in August, when the Indian agent called on the Auginash family, he found Jeanette home alone with the children. She reported that Fred was gone, that he was frustrated with the reservation and had "told his clan he was not coming back" to Red Lake. The agent immediately checked with Stayberg's Store in Redby and was relieved to learn that before departing Fred had put down the full amount of his recent check on the family's account. Clearly Jeanette had not represented her husband's real intentions to the agent. She knew the complete story—that Fred had only taken a vacation from the reservation and had already joined up with his White Earth relatives in Clearwater County for the ricing season.[20]

Jeanette's greatest desire in the early 1950s, according to my mother, was "to have her sons come home safely from the Army in Korea." In addition to worry about her sons, Fred, in his sixties, was in declining health and Jeanette too was recovering from an unspecified illness in the summer of 1949. It appears that in April 1948, after eighteen years, Fred had ended his job at the sawmill. Their two sons in the U.S. Army could no longer help their parents with fishing and other labor; Richard was stationed in distant Seattle and McKinley similarly far away in San Francisco. In 1949, the Auginash family's monthly income totaled $117. Fred received sixty dollars per month from the Veterans Administration, in addition to fifty-seven dollars in the form of an Aid to Dependent Children grant for his two daughters, in sixth and eighth grade. Jeanette, the inventive problem-solver, petitioned for a family allowance of fifty dollars per month to be taken from her sons' military paychecks, though it would be months before that issue was resolved. Further, Jeanette requested that the agency investigate the possibility that one of her sons could return home from the army in order to help out the family. At the time, the Red Lake superintendent agreed with her proposal, resulting in a flurry of official letters. He pointed out the agency's position, saying, "We feel that a discharge for one of the boys is very essential for the personal welfare of the family. Since both parents are now in poor health, such essential tasks as carrying water, splitting wood and shoveling snow are impossible for them." Further, he described the Auginash family's situation and present needs:

> The family live in a three-room house, which is well kept, clean, and neat but it is not modern and has no plumbing facilities, whatsoever, and the family must secure their water some distance from the house. Mr. Fred Auginash, father of the boys is in very poor health and he is unable to do even light work. During the past two months, Mrs. Auginash found herself in failing health and it appears unlikely that she will recover fully for many months.

Two children stay in the home, Florence, born 8/25/38, and Anna, born 9/6/35. The younger will be in the sixth grade in Redby, and the other will be in the eighth grade at the junior high school in Red Lake. Besides the boys there is only one other sibling. She is Mrs. Amelia Lussier, a housewife residing in Redby.[21]

The matter of the military family allowance grew more imperative when in 1950 Jeanette and Fred gained custody of their first grandchild, Gerald, who was Richard's two-year-old son. In April of that year Richard was stationed at Fort Riley, Kansas, prior to a stint in Alaska, and the agency wrote to him, saying, "Your mother advised that the boy has insufficient clothing and she does not have the funds to purchase any. We suggest, therefore, that you make a direct deduction from your pay and send it to your mother for the support of your son." By September, Richard had voluntarily increased an initial monthly allotment to his parents from twenty-five to forty dollars. With the escalation of the U.S conflict in Korea, neither Richard nor McKinley would return to the reservation until after their military service, and McKinley, in particular, was deeply entangled in the combat burden of war.[22]

On the reservation, it was often the case that grandparents became caretakers for their young family members just as ailments or chronic illness made an appearance. Still, women like Jeanette seemed eager to take on this very demanding role. When Jeanette's relative Mattie had a daughter on May 29, 1951, Jeanette soon became the full-time foster parent of her newborn girl, and an agreement was reached in the Court of Indian Offences by November, the same month Jeanette turned forty-six. It appears Mattie was leaving the reservation for relocation and to find work in California. In 1952, with Richard and McKinley both safely home from the war, the Auginash household budget consisted primarily of Fred's monthly sixty-three dollars in veteran's pension, supplemented by ADC for food and clothing for Anna (seventeen), Florence (fourteen), Gerald (four), and Barbara (one). Five years later, Jeanette would need to petition the reservation superintendent for twenty-five dollars from the "Individual Indian Accounts" for general living expenses for Barbara. In 1957, Jeanette and Fred achieved an important goal when they filed a petition of adoption for their grandson Gerald, which was approved by the General Council of the Red Lake Band of Chippewa Indians on August 4, 1957. Jeanette was fifty-one and Fred sixty-nine. On the document, Jeanette's elegant signature followed Fred's simple X.[23]

Gayaashk of Illinois

Something about my father reminded Grandpa Auginash of a gull. My mother suggested it was not at all because of his fair skin but rather his long neck, like the herring gulls of northern Minnesota, and neither she nor Grandpa Auginash possessed this interesting feature. Gayaashk was what the Auginash family first called Vernon David Child. These early conversations, of course, took place before my time, but still they represent what I have been told about the beginning of my parents' relationship and

Fred with Florence and Gerald, about 1950.

subsequent marriage on November 27, 1954. I have always considered my mother to have been shockingly young at the time, a mere sixteen to my father's relatively mature twenty-seven. However, to her new in-laws in Illinois, the most sobering detail of their son's choice of wife was not her age as much as her race.

That my parents ever met at all, let alone fell in love and married, is an unexpected story involving postwar mobility in the United States. In 1952, Vernon drove his green Fraser car to northern Minnesota to visit some distant relatives with the surname Mistic, and he worked for them a short time on their farm, which was adjacent to the southern border of the Red Lake Reservation. He had no background in agriculture other than a home garden plot, since his family in Illinois owned Child Motor Sales, a small business selling and repairing automobiles. My father had been drafted from his small town toward the end of World War II; made it as far as San Francisco, where he was stationed when he learned of the atomic bombs being dropped on Hiroshima and Nagasaki; and had attended some college on the GI Bill by the time he met my mother when she was a young teenager. He was bookish and always liked to point out various constellations and their Latin names, hence Grandpa Auginash's other nickname for him: Astronomy, as in, "Gagwejim *Astronomy* ji-wii-amwaad adikamegwan," or "Ask *Astronomy* if he would like some whitefish."[24]

My father was shy and quiet, considerably more stoic than my boisterous Ojibwe family, and deeply philosophical. He was, without question, the gentlest white man the Auginash family had ever met. Vernon studied English and history in college and was on his way to being a teacher. He carried around large anthologies for taking notes, though he was also an athlete. Early in his career he would combine teaching English with duties as a high school basketball coach. Life in downstate Illinois had cultivated in him a love of baseball and the St. Louis Cardinals, which he would one day pass on to his two children. From a family where every member had arrived in the Midwest from the north of England (and I have heard Yorkshire compared to Texas for its rural ways), he was the iconoclast as the only non-religious socialist. Until he left for the army, he had lived with his parents, Paul and Mabel Child, and his older brother and younger sister in the small Illinois town where both sets of his English immigrant grandparents also resided. The three siblings were redheads.

Once Vernon dared to drive his Fraser a few short miles across the boundary line of the Red Lake Indian Reservation, one of the first friendly young people he met was Florence, still a high school cheerleader. She was a contrast to him in every way possible— outgoing, pretty, funny, and rarely taking time to read a book. My mother remembered their first meeting as taking place in the winter of 1952, and she was immediately attracted, not so much to my father but rather to his "green Fraser with an Indian blanket on the front seat." The Navajo blanket was a souvenir from Vernon's wanderings in the West after the war, years when he wrote the following postcard home to his parents: "I came back to Tucson and I'm working as waiter-houseman at the Lodge on the Desert. I couldn't find anything to do in L.A. and union cards were too high in San Diego." Florence also suggested that when it became clear Vernon wished to marry her, her parents strongly approved; "My Dad and Mom liked Vernon," she said simply. Looking back in later years, Florence had mixed feelings about her readiness for marriage, suggesting that her parents and Vernon appeared to move very quickly and "they were talking about marriage, geez." Nevertheless, for the rest of her life she would consider her most important birthday to be "when I turned 16, so I could marry Vernon" and when "he asked me in March around his birthday we got engaged."[25]

Her Name is Florence

But before he married Florence, Vernon had to contemplate the place of an Indian wife in his own family. A few days before his birthday and engagement in 1954, he wrote a letter to his younger sister in Illinois, ruminating on what might be in store for him if

Vernon and Florence at the Auginash family home, Red Lake, 1954.

he married a young Indian woman, especially one from a poor family. Fortunately, my aunt Constance Finch held on to this very special letter for over forty years, eventually giving it to me in June 1996, the same month my father died. The letter is striking to me for several reasons, not least of which was the timing of its arrival in my own mailbox. It is incredibly charming to me to read a letter with the very first mention of my mother's name to my father's family. But the letter also reveals the innermost thoughts of a young, white, midwestern man at mid-century, one who is contemplating marriage to a woman of another race: in his words, "I know my situation is very unusual." Though he was a young man of twenty-six, I recognize my father immediately—I see the ethical sensibilities that guided his decisions, and his gentle turn of phrase.[26]

> Cass Lake, Minn., c/o Morris Landing, Route 2
> Dear Connie:
> I received your letter today and was very happy to get it. I read it before the other three letters I had,

as I wasn't sure who it was from. I feel that it was the most comforting and complimentary letter that I have ever received, and I am grateful for such thoughtful consideration.

When I wrote to this girl this morning (her name is Florence) I told her I considered myself very lucky to have a sister like you and a family who is so considerate of my welfare. You mentioned that mother was somewhat hurt at my not talking about things this summer or before I came up here. This summer there wasn't anything to talk about. I just knew her then.

I suppose it would be easier for you to accept her if she were white. Or would it? It's very hard to see another's viewpoint on that. She seems no different in that respect than anyone else to me. She is rather dark—though not exceptionally so. She has long black hair and I'm sure she would like you very much. I would like to be home, and I may be soon. I know my situation is very unusual, and sometimes I don't know what to do. I've often thought— like sitting at home on Sunday with everyone there— what would it be like? Do you think that she—if we were ever married—could be just like Shirley or Jerry [his siblings' spouses] in the family? Or would that be possible? It might seem very strange.

You see, she has never had much. She has told me at times that her folks think about her sometimes when she gets ragged. Her conditions have been pretty hard in many respects. If she had clothes like you or anyone else has, she would think it was out-of-this world. She told me the other day that she never expected to have anything or anyone, so what could you do with a girl like that, especially if you love her. It seems funny I suppose. I'll write again.

With love and thanks,
Vernon[27]

While on the one hand this is a very beautiful and sensitively rendered letter, my father's thoughtful words also indicate he was preparing for family disapproval—perhaps a cool reception of his "very unusual" marriage to Florence. In the small town to which Vernon always imagined returning, everyone was white and attitudes on race appeared fixed and well established. Moreover, in the 1950s intolerance was openly expressed, laws banning interracial marriage were upheld, and ideas of white supremacy and racial hierarchies compelled most Americans to strongly disapprove of marriages between whites and individuals of different races.

There were additional burdens to interracial couples in the 1950s in the shape of societal expectations, prejudice, and perhaps even law. Since the late nineteenth century, American Indians were included in a dozen state's laws prohibiting them from marriage to whites. Vernon's home state of Illinois was not one of these, since it had repealed all laws prohibiting interracial marriage in 1874, though the topic reemerged in an early twentieth-century controversy. Historian Peggy Pascoe argued that laws prohibiting interracial marriage were deeply embedded in U.S. history and "a project of white supremacy" and "America's longest-lasting form of legal race discrimination," even outlasting school segregation. Pascoe also dispelled the notion that measures meant to prevent interracial marriage steadily declined in the United States, pointing out that miscegenation laws actually escalated during the course of the first half of the twentieth century. In fact, the laws were bolstered by marriage licensing forms and procedures that as part of vital statistics asked applicants for information on race, a practice "which helped weave race and white supremacy throughout the American racial state."[28]

My mother's skin color, "dark—though not exceptionally so," would matter to the Child family but was not an issue to Beltrami County when she submitted an application for a marriage license in 1954. Florence Auginash and Vernon Child applied for a license in the city of Bemidji, but the forms they filled out did not ask them to declare their race, and Minnesota was in the minority of states for having no history of miscegenation law. In addition, Florence was free to marry since Minnesota statute allowed "every female person who has attained the full age of 16 years" to be married, making even parental consent unnecessary. Their original marriage certificate was signed by two witnesses, Jeanette and another individual who may have simply been an employee at the courthouse, since the ceremony took place in front of a municipal judge in Bemidji. My father recalled that Fred signed documents at the time with an X, and even though he was present for the ceremony, he was not an official witness. Florence remembered the pink dress she wore that day and that afterward Vernon took her and his new in-laws to dinner, the joy-fulness of the occasion somewhat overshadowed in his memory by the offense of his first experiences with the de facto segregation of Bemidji businesses in the 1950s, when Snider's Café was one of the few dining establishments to serve Indians.[29]

The Child family was working class but wealthy in comparison to Vernon's in-laws on the reservation. Through his marriage to Florence, Vernon brought the Auginash family some desperately needed resources and labor, even if he did not make formal offerings like those Fred had presented to David Jones in the 1920s, when my grandfather settled the Ojibwe obligations for establishing marriage with numerous gifts. Vernon had a reliable car and knew how to maintain it, which was no doubt incredibly helpful, and while he was never a hunter or fisherman like Fred, McKinley, or the men and women of Red Lake, he was willing to cut wood, haul water, paint, fix windows, run to the hardware store, or purchase groceries. From working in his own father's business, which also combined a gas station and auto repair shop, Vernon was handy, and to his credit he had a strong work ethic and appreciated physical labor. Vernon tackled their every home repair with enthusiasm, and Jeanette and Fred welcomed Vernon to the family. Despite their own versatile occupations and all-around hard work, in addition to significant contributions from their elder sons, Jeanette and Fred continued to struggle in poverty on the reservation. Their only financial security came in the form of Fred's steady pension check, now up to seventy-eight dollars a month. To Fred, Vernon's appearance on the reservation and marriage to his fun-loving daughter surely appeared as a stroke of luck.

Vernon had an additional talent. His college education and comfort with official business allowed him to set off in search of Fred's allotment. Fred insisted to his son-in-law that he owned land in Clearwater County, and according to the rolls of 1913, a man named Nahwahjewun indeed had allotment number 4830 on the White Earth Reservation. By the mid-1950s, the land would have only increased in value, and as an aging man with a young family, he needed the income. Vernon had heard Fred's entire story and knew of his original dispossession from Big Sandy Lake. It was always tragic to my father that, after searching through courthouse records, to his great regret he had to inform Fred that the land in Clearwater County had been seized by the state of Minnesota for nonpayment of taxes—taxes that were illegal in the first place. Nearly three decades after Fred's death, Minnesota and the U.S. Congress finally negotiated a settlement with the heirs of nineteen hundred allotments through the terms of the White Earth Reservation Land Settlement Act of 1985. It would be a few more years before my mother and her siblings received a small cash sum for Fred's allotment, since by that time Jeanette had also passed away.[30]

Another Accident and Aftermath

As Fred Auginash had decades before, Vernon found a genuine friend and ally in his Ojibwe father-in-law. Their bond continued a few short years, until Fred's death in 1957 and during which time the older man was often sick. Still, their relationship was of lifelong meaning to Vernon. Throughout the 1950s, Fred was in declining health and likely worried about Jeanette's future, especially with young children still in the household. As early as 1951,

Fred had been hospitalized several times, diagnosed by a Red Lake physician as having "conditions which disable him," including "hypertensive cardio-vascular disease, borderline diabetes, chronic osteo-arthritis of the spine, and a large post-operative hernia." At the time, his family hoped to take him to the Veterans Hospital in Fargo, though the senior physician at Red Lake "warned the family that this hospital may not wish to accept a patient with chronic disease," noting that "Mr. Auginash is, of course, unable to do much in the way of activity at his home and states that he feels better while in the hospital. This, of course, is to be expected. However, being essentially a chronic case, we hesitate to admit him here for prolonged care. We do not, however, object to admitting him for shorter periods to get him over some particular situation."[31]

Gerald Auginash would always remember Fred's appearance in his sixties, describing his grandfather as "short, hunched over, bowlegged" and saying "he always walked with his hands behind his back." Further, he noted that Grandpa Auginash "always wore long wool socks in winter, and something he called his 'squaw rubbers' on his feet, he also wore wool pants, buttoned up shirts, long johns and suspenders." He recalled that Fred "spoke Ojibwe" and was toward the end of his life "a grouchy old guy, though after church on Sundays he always enjoyed playing cards with his friend Al Morrison." Gerald easily summoned his memories of the day Grandpa Auginash died in 1957, an unusual summer for him as a nine-year-old boy since he was enjoying new friends, warm weather, and a few months of freedom with his uncle Vernon, who was working in Illinois. Gerald had taken a particular liking to Vernon's father, Paul Child, who was kind to children and made a point of telling him that he had access to the soda pop and candy bars sold in the gas station and garage. Gerald remembered the somber phone call they received from Florence, who was at home with her family on the reservation. After learning that Fred had died, he and Vernon immediately packed the car and left for northern Minnesota.

Jeanette and Fred Auginash with grandchildren Brian Child, right, and Wendell Cook, about 1957. This is the last picture of Grandpa Auginash.

The cause of her father's death always made Florence terribly sad, and I was in college before she gave me an anguished account of how Fred died of an accidental poisoning. It was a simple story. Prior to the events surrounding his death, the fact that Fred insisted on speaking Ojibwe with his wife and children was always a positive statement of cultural pride for my mother, one that I enjoyed hearing. Florence often told me that whenever as a girl she returned home from school speaking English to her parents, her father would always gently reprimand, in her words, "now say that to me in Indian." My mother recounted that Grandpa Auginash had recently been to the doctor and received two identical bottles of medicine, one of which was a topical liniment intended to relieve arthritis. He awoke very early one morning in late July, just a few days before the council was to finalize Gerald's adoption, and, unable to read the label, drank the wrong bottle of medicine. Vernon and Gerald arrived on the reservation in time to observe his body being taken from the house through a window, a Midewiwin practice, followed by four days of ceremonies, the family in the end blending these Ojibwe traditions with his burial in the Catholic cemetery. Two brief notes from the Red Lake Agency during the summer of 1957 mention that "Fred Auginash died 7–26–57 of metaylsalicylate poisoning" and "Jeanette receives money from the Veteran's Administration."[32]

After Fred's death, Jeanette received a reduced pension from the Veterans Administration amounting to sixty-seven dollars per month for her and Gerald, and she continued to receive $17.50 in ADC, since she still had custody of toddler Barbara. "After Fred was gone, we depended on McKinley for wood in the winter. He had a truck, chainsaws, and he would bring the wood over. I split wood and carried it inside," recalled Gerald, describing the main concern of reservation households in northern Minnesota in the days of wood stoves. When Gerald reached his teens, the family often resorted to a different strategy for winter survival: he spent the season on the reservation with his father, Richard, as Jeanette visited her married daughter in Illinois. By the time he was in high school, they were still surviving through Jeanette's fishing and liquor sales and Fred's pension, and as Gerald recalled with hollow laughter, "Sometimes I had to cut down a tree after basketball practice" just to heat the house.[33]

If marriage marks the beginning of a new life, it was especially so for Florence, since she had limited experience with white society. Naturally, she worried that she would not find acceptance once she left the reservation, and thus her first impressions of the unfamiliar ways of her husband's family were exceptionally significant. As the year turned to spring and warmer weather, they headed south in the green Fraser, and "We went home to Illinois to see his parents for the first time." After a long car trip from northern Minnesota, the couple arrived in Vernon's small town to find his mother outside working her garden, wearing a large straw hat to protect her graying red hair and fair skin. The Child home in western Illinois was simple and modest, with a large green yard of apple and cherry trees, a path of long winding vines of concord grapes, and patches of asparagus and strawberries in addition to the vegetable garden. Directly across the street was a well-built, two-story Victorian home with a wide front porch and swing—all constructed by Vernon's grandfather, James Child, around 1910. Vernon's elderly grandmother Elizabeth still lived there with her daughter, Amy, who tended the English flower beds and walnut trees. The Child women gave Florence and Vernon an affectionate and very warm welcome home.[34]

In the following days, Florence would be amazed at her mother-in-law's bounty of fresh food and considerable cooking skills, in a household where every noodle was lovingly made by hand. She noticed that Mabel was a superb housewife who adored cooking for her family but hated to clean up the kitchen afterward, and so Florence enjoyed helping out with the dishes and in this way they formed a bond. It was easy for Florence to return Mabel's genuine affection. Still, I suspect every family has a weak spot, an imperfection that disturbs or concerns some members more than others, and with the audacity to show up on holidays.

Florence's new father-in-law, Paul Child, while never ceasing to be a pleasant gentleman, would remain more distant, far more conflicted about his son's marriage than his wife. This tension would grow into a weak spot in our larger family relations—only in an ideal world is it enough that a fine, young couple comes together without bias—and racism hurts even those you love. I always knew the weak spot. As a young girl in elementary school, I remember Grandpa Child's occasional discourses on race and attempts to add up my own blood quantum in a way that was satisfactory to him, never failing to point out my English ancestry. His deepest hope rested in genealogy, and if my mother had even one European somewhere in the family tree—he thought perhaps a wandering Frenchman in the Great Lakes—the balance would tip in his favor. He even knew that Jeanette, whom the Childs always referred to rather formally as "Mrs. Auginash," was enrolled as a "full-blood," and so it was that my late Grandpa Auginash became Grandpa Child's more likely candidate for this French ancestor.

Paul Child was never—if this is even possible—an *obnoxious* racist, though he held views on race and white supremacy entrenched among his white, working-class generation. Like his wife, he was the offspring of fairly recent English immigrants, the first in their families to be born in the United States. Our talks on race took place in the 1960s, and since I knew Grandpa Child was born in 1903, he appeared to me sadly behind the times. His ideas never bothered or persuaded me since I knew he was wrong and I always liked being Indian.

These early and unfortunate conversations gave me a deeper understanding of racial struggle in the United States, but the weak spot in my family also accounts for my optimism, especially regarding the ability of good people to eventually attempt to overcome difference. In another historic car trip, in July 1962, Mabel and Paul visited the Auginash family and our Ojibwe homelands on the Red Lake Reservation. The events of that visit form some of my earliest childhood memories and are among my few strong recollections of Grandma Child. Not long after the trip to northern Minnesota, Mabel suffered a debilitating stroke from which she never recovered, passing away in the summer of 1965. As Mabel and Paul's youngest grandchild, I grew especially close to my grandfather during her long illness. He remained a widower for the rest of his life, until his own death at eighty-eight. Grandpa Child was the security blanket of my childhood, and I never doubted his kind heart or devotion to me or my brother. To borrow a phrase from my father's letter, I have always considered myself very lucky to have a family so considerate of my welfare. The respect that grew between members of the Auginash and Child families after 1954, despite early years of uncertainty, now appears permanent.

In later years, and well after Fred's death, my father rarely referred to Grandpa Auginash by name, instead calling him "the old man," but in an Ojibwe sense, where it is a sign of deep respect. I learned about Grandpa Auginash from both my mother and father, and now from writing this history of his work and marriage. My mother liked to tell a little amusing story of the time Jeanette and Fred visited her in Illinois, when she was newly married and my father was working as a schoolteacher in another small town. Vernon drove the family from northern Minnesota, stopping at a restaurant along the way. Florence ordered fish for her father, hoping he would like a familiar dish. She always laughed remembering how he ate the fish and politely saved the tiny dish of tartar sauce for dessert. My father's most endearing story about Fred took place later in this memorable visit, when Vernon was back at work. He happened to glance out the schoolhouse window during class and was very surprised to see his father-in-law picking up paper and cleaning the school yard, wanting to be helpful at Vernon's place of employment. I still wonder about the nature of their relationship because communication was imperfect, yet it is finally clear to me they had created a mutual respect from their shared belief that labor is the best way to care for and express your love of family. When my father retired and built a new house with my mother on Jeanette's land across the river, he frequently spoke of his memories of Fred, and always with great emotion. As a former teacher with an appreciation for good literature, he once told me how much the character of Eli in Louise Erdrich's *Love Medicine,* one of his favorite books, reminded him of "the old man."

Jeanette died on February 1, 1987, three full decades after Fred's death, though she was seldom alone, always spending time in the company of friends, relatives, and grandchildren, a number of whom she raised. More than a matriarch to our large extended family and her twenty-nine grandchildren, she was simply the edifice upon which everyone else's peace and happiness rested. In my ignorance while growing up, I never once thought of Grandma Auginash as having an occupation. I certainly observed her working, doing tasks that might be simple today, like laundry, but that were an ordeal in a home without running water. Throughout the 1960s, Redby residents continued to haul their fresh springwater home from the fishery in large milk cans. Grandma Auginash did not have a bathroom or running water in her home until she moved into an apartment building for the elderly on the reservation during the 1970s. Soon after, on her land across the river in Redby, a HUD house with just three rooms but all the amenities was built for her. Looking back at her younger life and my grandparents' marriage, I now see what a force Jeanette was in that relationship and to her family's survival on the Red Lake Reservation.[35]

It is a challenge to even try to represent the full extent of Jeanette's and Fred's labor, or to demonstrate the daily strategic decisions that shaped their reservation existence, but by placing some of our family's stories and reminiscences alongside tribal records, government archives, and other documents, their incredibly productive working lives come into greater focus. The following chapters investigate changes in labor practices on the reservation—fishing, healing, and ricing—activities that were and are essential work of the Ojibwe people. I am proud to think of Jeanette as a fisherwoman, one of her many roles.

FAMILIES AT WORK
■ ■ ■ ■

3

An Ojibwe Fishery Story
Ojibwe Labor during World War I

M y ancestors and family have fished the waters of Upper and Lower Red Lake, one of the largest freshwater lakes in the United States, for centuries, and our relationship to this lake is an enduring legacy from earlier generations of Anishinaabeg. We fished the waters of Upper and Lower Red Lake when the United States was a nascent country working to draw up legal documents of confederation; and we still fished there when European settlers moved into Minnesota during the 1830s; and we continued to do so once Minnesota became a state in 1858. Our fishing never ceased once we negotiated for our reservation. At Red Lake and other Ojibwe communities along the U.S. and Canadian border, the day-to-day working lives of Ojibwe women, men, and their families revolved around fishing activities—making nets, maintaining boats, observing weather, setting nets or spearing fish, removing fish from nets, and preserving fish, or in later years bringing it in for marketing. Since ice fishing was important to winter survival, it was work that continued throughout every season. Walleye, whitefish, pickerel, perch, and other fish sustained our people.

Our relationship to Upper and Lower Red Lake remains undiminished after all these years, even in the aftermath of the Agreement of 1889, when government surveys fraudulently sliced off a portion of the eastern upper lake. Our people remember that the hereditary chiefs never agreed to less than the entirety of the lake, and we stand with our ancestors in our insistence that the whole of Upper Red Lake belongs to the Ojibwe people by right of aboriginal title and federal agreement, in addition to being our sacred responsibility. Yet the story of how state and federal authorities have grasped for control over our waters persists as a decades-long narrative of struggle.

Harvesting fish has been a long-standing point of contention between tribes and states, especially after the establishment of new administrative offices that sought to be the sole authority over Indigenous and non-Indigenous citizens and their relationship to game, fish, and other natural resources. The Minnesota state government's first major grab of Red Lake's fish started in 1917, when the state fishery was instituted at Red Lake as an emergency effort to ease food shortages for the people of Minnesota during the crisis of World War I. By 1929, when a new agreement was negotiated between Red Lake and the state, the fishery had matured into a profitable business, so that a surplus of funds sat in the state treasury. That same year, Red Lake people decided to establish a fishery cooperative on the reservation, and my grandmother and her father, David Jones, were early members.[1]

A Red Lake woman participating in commercial fishing, 1941.

But once again, the trust responsibility of the federal government toward an Indian tribe would be ignored in favor of state profits and greater access to Indigenous resources. While Red Lake fisher men and women harvested the fish and delivered them to the state fishery for processing, a large portion of the profits went directly into the state treasury. For the next decade, the state of Minnesota was involved in a circle of dubious activities in the contested region of Upper Red Lake, where it had used Red Lake's contributions to the fish fund from the state's treasury to purchase land near the Tamarac River as well as buildings in the village of Waskish. So not only were tribal members being denied access to the eastern portion of Upper Red Lake, they were compelled through their labor to pay the state of Minnesota so it could deny that access. This action was outrageous and duplicitous on Minnesota's part.

Fisher Men and Women

Dakota writer and physician Charles Eastman toured Ojibwe Country in the years prior to World War I, traveling the backwoods and lakes of northern Minnesota and Ontario and composing his impressions of the Ojibwe seasonal economy:

> Their craftsmanship is as simple as it is ingenious, and
> nearly everything they use is made by themselves, lov-
> ingly, and with patient skill. Years ago all their fish-nets
> were of the wild hemp, but now they use twine bought at
> the trading-posts. I saw the women at work making them
> in different sizes for catching different kinds of fish. Two
> light, thin, cedar strips are used for netting, one about
> two inches square, the other from five to eight inches
> long with a rounded point, slit to form a tongue. When
> thirty yards or so are made, it is weighted with stones,
> and strips of cedar wood are tied to the upper edge as
> floaters. These white floaters are noticeable along the

shallows and wooded shores of the lakes, and in the
early morning it is common to see the women, together
or singly, lifting their nets and taking the catch into the
canoes.[2]

After finding similar labor practices in several of the communities he visited, and being impressed by the proficiency of
men and women at work, Eastman summed up his admiration:
"These people actually live by hunting and fishing, wild rice and
berry gathering, and no country could be more perfectly adapted
to such a life."[3]

One of the most influential commentators on American Indian
life in the early twentieth century, Eastman nonetheless glossed
over the difficult circumstances Indigenous people were negoti-
ating in favor of uplifting stories, seeking only to portray Indians
in the most positive light possible to his readers. He charmingly
described an Ojibwe seasonal economy without a single reference
to economic crisis, limiting his consideration to Ojibwe work
roles, tools, and equipment, while frequently calling attention to
the work of women. Had Eastman traveled farther south to the
White Earth Reservation, he would have found it impossible to
avoid witnessing Ojibwe people struggling to survive an enormous dispossession, but because of his more northerly itinerary,
he was able to experience a still-functioning seasonal economy.
He wrote, "Each season of the year has its characteristic occupation. In the early fall they fish with nets at the outlets of the large
lakes or in the narrows between their countless islands, sometimes spearing the fish by torchlight. The flesh is cut into thin
strips and smoked or sun-dried. At this time they shot many ducks
and cure them in the same way for winter use."

Eastman was a finely tuned ethnographer, having himself
lived a seasonal way of life within the diasporic Dakota communities of Minnesota and Manitoba, and as he once said of his own
childhood in his book *Indian Boyhood,* "we were close students of
nature." Accordingly, Eastman profoundly appreciated the supe-

rior skills involved in Ojibwe fishing, and that no labor was more essential to them.[4]

Red Lake men, women, and their families had always organized the labor of fishing. Fishing required "patient skill" and an ability to make fish nets of wild hemp or store-bought twine. At Red Lake and many other Ojibwe communities, fishing labor allowed families and other small collectives of relatives or friends to set up seasonal fish camps and work together near the lakes in warmer weather, an older practice that continued at Red Lake throughout the 1950s. Frances Densmore, the Minnesota ethnologist and a contemporary of Eastman, explained that for the Ojibwe, "Fishing was an industry which continued almost the entire year," from right after the spring maple sugar camps through the ice fishing season. Densmore, like Eastman, observed the activity of women in fishing labor. While Densmore's writings also portray the essential activities of men in spear fishing and ice fishing, she noted, "Fishing, except in the coldest winter, was the work of the women, who placed the nets in the water at night and took them up in the early morning, spreading and drying them."[5]

No Trespassing

Once they saw the bounty that Ojibwe people were harvesting from the lakes, non-Indian visitors and settlers on the border and in other regions of Minnesota immediately sought to appropriate Indigenous resources, creating new struggles in the twentieth century over treaty rights and access to fish and leading to the modern crises of invasive species, overfishing, and pollution. Ojibwe fisher men and women in the Great Lakes and Mississippi River region, along with their leaders, fought multiple battles to maintain their right to fish. For the population of approximately two thousand people who lived and worked on the Red Lake Reservation in the early twentieth century, community survival depended on waging a steady battle against a determined federal government still drawing up plans to allot the reservation

Removing fish from nets, about 1935.

throughout the 1920s. They also faced a very real threat presented by the state of Minnesota, which aspired to one day soon take control of the largest freshwater lake (apart from Superior) in the state. The faulty mapping at the turn of the century, which deliberately failed to represent the reservation's correct boundaries, was just the first step.[6]

Moreover, the people of Red Lake and its hereditary chiefs, not to mention tribal officials on the reservation and legal associates, had to thwart the steady overtures of ordinary Minnesota citizens who never lost a desire to fish in Red Lake. When the state of Minnesota began to operate a fishery at Red Lake during World War I, Minnesota and its citizens were first in line to benefit economically from Indigenous resources and labor. The needs and income of Ojibwe fisher men and women were of secondary consideration. For the most part, non-Indian competitors for the land and abundant waters of the Red Lake Reservation believed it was simply a matter of time before the entirety of Upper and Lower Red Lake would be fully opened to them.

By the time of World War I, the entire ecosystem of Upper and Lower Red Lake was the lifeblood and economic strength of the Ojibwe women, men, and families who lived on the reservation. The need to protect their land and water and its resources also played a role in the decision at Red Lake to adopt a written constitution in 1918, which reaffirmed their separate political status from other Ojibwe and their decision to "not recognize the General Council of the Minnesota Chippewas, as a medium for the transaction of their tribal property and business." Politicians in Minnesota planned to merge Red Lake's tribal funds with those of other Ojibwe within the state, especially as land and timber was sold and exploited. This volatile situation was deeply troubling to Red Lake's self-governing communities, whose members had much to fear in the aftermath of the all-out plunder of the White Earth Reservation, making autonomy their only logical political strategy.[7]

Because the leaders preserved the Red Lake homeland and because they also succeeded in resisting allotment, the Red Lake Band's political, cultural, and social history reflect a remarkable legacy within the broader story of American Indians in the twentieth century. The consistent political message of the hereditary chiefs and other leaders was this: they had a separate identity and political status from the other Ojibwe bands, even as the federal government wished to view all the Ojibwe people in the state of Minnesota as a single political entity.

The hereditary chiefs also diligently and doggedly pursued non-Indians who trespassed onto their land and lakes—a challenging task considering that a large part of the reservation's border was water. In one documented example of hereditary chiefs policing reservation borders, in 1907 an American photographer named Roland Reed entered the Red Lake homelands determined to take pictures of the Ojibwe in ways that would have lasting "historical value." Born in Wisconsin like his contemporary Edward Curtis, Reed felt entitled to traverse the reservation's border, blithely unconcerned with the consequences his presence or mission might provoke. Red Lake's hereditary chiefs, spread over many villages across the reservation, shared responsibility for dealing with trespassers for the protection of their communities.

Reed was immediately confronted by King Bird, one of the chiefs who watched over the east side of Red Lake, who told him, according to Reed, to "get out at once and not come back." The Red Lake leaders' strategy to immediately confront trespassers was an extraordinarily simple and long-standing expression of their sovereignty, one more necessary than ever at a time when missionaries, teachers, government workers, and illicit loggers and fishermen regularly intruded on the reservation. Like these other unwanted visitors, Reed was determined to complete his mission, and his short stay at Red Lake allowed him, in the end, to entice subjects to pose in feathers and blankets for the attractive sum of ten dollars. Having made their point, the chiefs later viewed Reed's presence in the community as nonthreatening, and his Red Lake photographs eventually became popular on tourist postcards.[8]

The Agreement of 1889 and Its Aftermath

In historical documents about the Red Lake Ojibwe during the nineteenth century, Medweganoonind is often referred to as the respected "old chief." In his fifties when he signed the treaty of 1863, he later took part in several Ojibwe delegations to Washington. He was the head hereditary chief among the seven chiefs who negotiated the Agreement of 1889, when he was reportedly eighty-two years old. Medweganoonind was from the community of Redby on the south side of Lower Red Lake. He is remembered today as a determined advocate on behalf of the Red Lake people who weathered an extraordinarily difficult era, and as a visionary who at every turn adamantly opposed the allotment of the reservation. Though Medweganoonind spoke the Ojibwe language, his eloquence and even his sense of humor are easily discerned throughout the translated negotiations that preceded the signing of the Agreement of 1889. He objected most strongly to the ideas of Knute Nelson, the Minnesota senator who had introduced the consolidation and allotment legislation in St. Paul and whom Medweganoonind and the other chiefs insisted on referring to as "Ground Squirrel."[9]

The Minnesota committee appointed to carry out the work of the Nelson Act included former trader and Minnesota senator Henry M. Rice, who chaired the U.S. Chippewa Commission. The Nelson Act called for removal of many Ojibwe bands from their homelands, cession of surplus lands, and allotment of Ojibwe reservations. At Red Lake in June and July of 1889, Medweganoonind specifically addressed Rice and the commissioners about the constant intrusions onto Red Lake lands, the timber fires set by settlers (who faced no legal consequences by harvesting damaged timber), and the overall unfeasibility of the allotment plan. Ojibwe diplomats were accustomed to express concern about the welfare of future generations, and Medweganoonind spoke of his descendants at Red Lake and urged the gathering to allow the decision to rest with the older men, as was protocol at Red Lake.

The Rice Commission, and member Bishop Martin Marty in particular, called for a two-thirds vote of all males over the age of eighteen, hoping to sway individual opinion, if not that of the hereditary chiefs, toward a new agreement. Medweganoonind addressed the assembled Red Lake community in the following way:

My friends, it is well to meet the commission understandingly. You can not be blamed on account of your ignorance for taking different positions. For my part, I am getting aged; I see that I shall be called upon by the Master of Life to deliver an account of myself. I cannot sacrifice your interests on account of my feelings. At my age I must do as my fathers have done; I must look to my grand children and their children's grandchildren; I must look after the benefit of all. I shall be dead when you receive the benefits of this work. If it pleases the Master of Life that this should be a blessing to us, it will be because we follow the advice of those who are sent to

us, and who say they are our special friends. I do not want
to hide anything; I want to give a fair expression of my
views. I want to reserve enough land here, if the commissioners will consent and the arrangement is concluded.
If not, we must persevere and try to gain our point. It is
to our interest to do so, as, if we make a mistake, it is for
a lifetime. I will ask you to be patient. We are willing to
make an arrangement, but we must be very careful and
make no mistake. Speak carefully to the commission.
Let nothing mar our intercourse, I beg that of you.

Medweganoonind then addressed the Rice Commission, emphasizing Red Lake's consistent position of independence from the
other Ojibwe bands in Minnesota, who were not faring well with
removal and allotment. He spoke: "It is our wish that there be
no consolidation, but whatever we get here we should get alone.
That we should receive, solely, the profits of our reservation. We
want an expression of your views again. We don't wish that your
mission here should be a failure. We wish it to be a success. We
wish to hear once more about receiving ourselves the proceeds
of our own land."[10]

When on July 6, 1889, the Red Lake leaders signed an agreement for a reduced reservation, the land continued to be held in
common, as Medweganoonind wished. After the ranked hereditary chiefs, 247 Red Lake men signed the Agreement of 1889, but
it was Medweganoonind who went first and whose words to the
Rice Commission are still recalled: "This property under discussion, called Red Lake, is my property. These persons whom you
see before you are my children. They own this place the same as
I own it. My friends, I ask that we reserve the whole of the lake
as ours and that of our grandchildren hereafter . . . I will never
consent to the allotment plan. I wish to lay out a reservation here,
where we can remain with our bands forever." Medweganoonind's words underscore the understanding at Red Lake *"to reserve
the whole of the lake as ours."*[11]

While on the one hand Red Lake's challenge to the state of Minnesota and the United States is an amazing success story during the period of reservation allotment and cultural assimilation, for the people of Red Lake the loss of several million acres and the arrival of new settlers on their former hunting, farming, and gathering lands represented a new era, one that meant greater poverty and less freedom. It is only in hindsight that we look at the negotiation as one that helped Red Lake maintain land and sovereignty. Later in the summer of 1889, a letter addressed to the U.S. commissioner Thomas J. Morgan from the Indian agent in Brainerd gave "a brief state of their present condition." The agent described the Red Lake Reservation as having "uninhabitable" government buildings and a sawmill "in hopeless ruin." Red Lake people continued to ask for assistance from the government, and their agent in Brainerd reported, "Although surrounded by pine forests, they have not boards enough to make coffins for the dead. Their houses are in dilapidated condition, and for the want of material cannot be repaired." Another land cession, of western townships, in 1902 further reduced resources and land available to the people of Red Lake, especially for one settlement of Ojibwe who lived on the property. Later, in 1916, 100,000 acres of Red Lake white pine were opened to logging under the U.S. secretary of interior's direction.[12]

Through these years, Red Lake's leaders continued their vigilance. Praying Day, one of the hereditary chiefs who signed the Agreement of 1889, contacted the Indian Agency at Leech Lake in the spring of 1900 to urge the agent there to write on his behalf to the commissioner of Indian Affairs, in Washington, DC. Praying Day was concerned about new practices within Minnesota that infringed on Ojibwe waters. The agent explained to the commissioner, "With reference to previous correspondence on the subject, I have the honor to transmit herewith a letter from Praying day (Ah num e ay ke zhig) concerning fishing licenses in the waters belonging to the Red Lake Reservation." The Red Lake Ojibwe were seeking damages "which they believe themselves entitled to" and had also made claims "against the State of Minnesota for granting licenses to the citizens of the State to fish in the water of the Lake of the Woods" in years past, prior to American settlement of the region. Praying Day's complaint to Washington shows the consistency of Red Lake leaders who established an early policy of defending their water as well as their land when dealing with Minnesota and its citizens.[13]

Fishing in World War I and the early 1920s

The state fishery at Red Lake was established in 1917 by the Minnesota Commission of Public Safety, an organization invested with broad powers during World War I to protect, defend, and apply the state's resources for a successful end to the war. The commission is better remembered for regulating morality, barring foreign language use in the classroom, and registering "aliens," who were prohibited from working as schoolteachers. State fisheries, including the one at Red Lake, were advanced in Minnesota based on the necessity of providing a fresh source of fish to the public during a period of wartime food conservation and as an alternative to meat. Of the state fisheries established during the war, though, only one was built on Indian land.[14]

Among the many changes brought by the state fishery was one in a fundamental recognition of just who was doing the work, as American culture often failed to comprehend Indigenous women's labor. The common use of the English word *fisherman* throughout the United States is a convention that appears to erase the history of women's fishing labor in the Great Lakes and Mississippi River region. But as Eastman and Densmore agreed, women "together or singly" were active in the Ojibwe traditional fishing economy. Linguist John Nichols explains that "occupational terms" are relatively new, but "the Ojibwe language varieties offer three ways of creating agent nouns to refer to people who do things such as fish" yet "the verbs underlying them identify specific fishing techniques." Consequently, Ojibwe terms for "fishes with a net,"

The state fishery, Red Lake, about 1917.

bagida'waa, or "cleans fish," bakazhaawe, or "goes fishing," nooji-giigoonyiwe, tend to be gender neutral. As Nichols points out, in recent years the Ojibwe language has incorporated some English patterns, so that "most speakers today will freely create feminine forms for all occupations" perceived as male, yet still use begida'waawaad for "anyone seen setting a net."[15]

When the new state fishery was formed at Red Lake in 1917, and Ojibwe fishing was transformed overnight into part of a state and regional economy, documents and photographs indicate that women continued to participate in fishing labor. Still, the language of official reports consistently referred to "fishermen" at Red Lake. In 1925, the commercial fishing season commenced on July 10 and continued through most of the month of November. At that time, according to a report compiled by superintendent S. A. Selvog of the Minnesota State Fisheries, who was stationed on the reservation, "Ice formed along the shores to such an extent that boats no longer could be operated. Many nets were lost in the drifting ice, and the *Indian fishermen* [emphasis added] were hard hit."[16]

Commercial fishing swiftly emerged on the reservation after construction of the Minnesota State Fisheries in Redby, as the state entered into an agreement with the federal government and the Red Lake Band of Chippewa to produce fish for the public during a period of wartime shortages. The new business was facilitated by the earlier era of lumbering, since in the decade after the Nelson Act the Minneapolis, Red Lake and Manitoba rail line had been constructed in this remote area of southern Beltrami County to fully exploit the massive pine timber and move it to markets off the reservation. The rail line was close to the south shore of Red Lake in the village of Redby, the site of the state fishery and the origin of the thirty-mile track that led to Bemidji. The change was dramatic for the fisher men and women of Red Lake. In 1918, 500,000 pounds of fish were harvested and shipped from the fishery in Redby, first on to Bemidji by rail, and then to various places in Minnesota.[17]

Fish harvests from Upper and Lower Red Lake continued to be significant. Every year throughout the 1920s, several hundred thousand pounds of Red Lake walleye, whitefish, pickerel, perch, and other fish in lots as large as one hundred pounds left Redby in refrigerator cars headed for markets in Minneapolis. After 1921, fish could be shipped out of state, and Chicago became a destination. Salted and smoked fish were also shipped by freight or by parcel post in ten-pound cartons. Orders were taken directly in Redby, where the fisheries offices were maintained during the season and where Superintendent Selvog managed business. In the five-year contract negotiated in January 1924 between Selvog and Game and Fish commissioner for the state of Minnesota James F. Gould, along with commissioner of Indian Affairs Charles H. Burke, the upper limit of fish to be taken from Red Lake was set at "not more than six hundred fifty thousand (650,000) pounds of fish" during any one fishing season—though the limit was exceeded.[18]

Red Lake fisher men and women were limited to producing fish only for the Minnesota State Fisheries operated by the state Game and Fish Department. Since the fishery operation was administered by the state, those who fished were "required to obtain permits from the Indian office and provide themselves with such equipment as is required," and it was the state that specified the size of mesh that could be used.[19]

The price of the fish procured by Red Lake fisher men and

Ice harvested from the lake in winter was used to preserve the catch through summer months, about 1935.

women was determined in Minnesota's Game and Fish Department's contract with the Bureau of Indian Affairs, since it began as a wartime measure for Minnesota residents, and prevailing market prices were not paid to workers or the tribe, even after the war ended. Individual fisher men and women were paid by the pound for the fish they produced, with whitefish at six cents per pound and pike at five cents per pound. In addition, a royalty went to the whole band at the end of the fishing season.[20]

This monopoly secured by the U.S. government effectively banned Red Lake people from taking part in further commercial fishing and deriving income from their own lake. Still, there were constant inquiries from the public about Red Lake's supply of fish. In 1925, one Minnesota businessman wrote to the Indian agent on the reservation asking, "Would it be legal for an outsider to go in there and deal with these Indian for these fish for the purposes of reselling them either retail or wholesale?" The rules governing Red Lake commercial fishing were laid out by the state's Game and Fish commissioner in a 1926 letter to a businessman from Warroad, Minnesota, who hoped to purchase fish directly from Red Lake. Commissioner Gould explicitly stated that Red Lake Indians who fish commercially did so "under a treaty or contract between the Bureau of Indian Affairs and the Game and Fish Department of Minnesota." This contract "specifies just what the annual production shall be from the waters of Red lake and that all fish produced by the Indians" must be then "sold to the Minnesota State Fisheries operated by the State Game and Fish Department," which also "stipulates the minimum price which the state shall pay." Commissioner Gould underscored the restrictions placed on Ojibwe commercial fishing:

> The Indians have no legal right to fish commercially in the waters of Red Lake further than their own personal or family consumption and the moment they fish in the waters of Red lake and attempt or do transport fish produced by them outside the confines of the Indian reservation for sale to you or any other company, both the seller and the purchaser subject themselves to prosecution under game and fish laws for sale and buying game fish and other species produced, sold, or bought illegally or in other words, other than by a license or contract. I urge you not to purchase any fish from these Red Lake Indians and furthermore, sincerely hope that in the event you refuse to buy such fish and you learn of anyone else at Warroad who does, that you will be kind enough to inform me as to their identity.[21]

The state fishery at Red Lake operated much as other business enterprises on Indian reservations in the United States, where the government, in this case the state of Minnesota and its citizens, was first in line to benefit economically from Indigenous resources and labor. Of secondary importance was the ability to make a living or the interests of Red Lake fisher men and women.

A non-Indian was hired as a "fish-hauler" to do business on the reservation, though a more poorly paid "fish weigher" might be an Indian employee, "if practicable," according to Washington. Superintendent Selvog, in charge of overseeing the Redby fishery for the state, acknowledged the Ojibwe frustration with state management: that "the price paid for the same quality of fish is much under that paid by private parties cannot be questioned," he wrote, and "this in itself results in dissatisfaction on the part of the Indians." Publicly, however, Selvog reported to the Bemidji newspaper that the Indians were well paid "over contract" for their labor. Interestingly, Selvog himself believed in their economic autonomy and that the Red Lake Ojibwe had the right to "carry on fishing without the sanction of this Department and irrespective of the laws of the State of Minnesota," though his position was never seriously considered in St. Paul.[22]

The state fishery, while providing essential income to working men and women at Red Lake, was also a source of continual friction. Since the state fishery originated as a wartime measure, "every pound of fish produced from the waters of Red Lake in the State of Minnesota" was to "make it possible for Minnesota residents to secure the fish at lower prices," even after the end of the war. In addition, the state fishery was unpopular with fish wholesalers and meat dealers within Minnesota, who disliked the competition posed by the Red Lake Fisheries, even adopting a resolution for the state to "go out of the fishing business."[23]

The state fishery operated under an ecologically unsound assumption that the supply of fish in Upper and Lower Red Lake was unlimited, indeed even overly abundant. In 1925 Selvog tapped into two controversies in a revealing article for *Fins, Feathers and Fur*, the magazine published by the Minnesota State Fisheries Game and Fish Department. First, he discussed the extent of the decline of "fish resources" at Red Lake due to the impact of a state fishery but dismissed the idea of overfishing, suggesting that "natural reproduction and artificial propagation" would offset the 849,512 pounds of fish that were taken from Upper and

Weighing the day's fish catch, about 1935.

Lower Red Lake during the 1925 season. Typical of "conservation" practices in the early twentieth-century United States, the fisheries manager saw no need to proceed with caution or concern for the future, since he believed there was the potential for "indefinite production" at Red Lake. Selvog also alluded to an existing controversy against the state fishery from commercial competitors who believed "these fish should not be taken for the purpose of marketing the same, *and should be preserved for the sportsmen and the tourists.*" In 1926 Commissioner Gould himself reported to the Minnesota legislature that Upper and Lower Red Lake was ripe for unlimited harvest as he presented preposterous information that before commercial fishing, under Ojibwe management, it was "overpopulated with fish life."[24]

In 1926 the commissioner of Indian Affairs described the "mutual advantage" to the Red Lake Indians and Minnesota and the relationship's success. That same year Commissioner Gould commented on a legal issue—whether the Red Lake Ojibwe must comply with state laws over hunting and fishing in light of the U.S. federal law declaring Indian citizenship. Most Indians in the United States had become citizens with the taking of allotments, and since Red Lake had never been allotted, its residents were a large block of new citizens in Indian Country. Gould wrote, "The Red Lake Indian Reservation happens to be the only existent full-fledged Indian Reservation in the State of Minnesota today, and, under Indian Treaty laws and Supreme Court decisions, Indian[s] may hunt and fish in season and out of season, on such reservations, but may not take thereon anything out of season and market the same outside the reservation."[25]

Gould was unequivocal in his understanding of the Ojibwe right to hunt and fish on the reservation, but problems remained. The fisher men and women of Red Lake lived in a new era of commercial fishing, but they continued to engage in other fishing labor year-round to support their families. They worried about the non-Indians who fished along that small stretch of Upper Red Lake at Waskish, wrongly designated as beyond the boundaries of the reservation; they were also allowed to sell the fish they caught to the state. Most troubling of all to Red Lake fisher men and women who ushered in commercial fishing, they no longer completely organized their own labor or controlled the entirety of the upper lake.[26]

Testing the Legal Waters

In the fall of 1926, the Red Lake Band retained a lawyer, Edward L. Rogers, from the town of Walker, Minnesota, "to compel the state to pay market prices for their fish," and drew up plans with him to take part in a test case to see if they might sell their own fish off the reservation. When the band's lawyer informed Commissioner Gould of the plan, he responded with a heavy hand. Not only did Gould threaten with arrest "any Indian found selling or offering for sale outside the confines of the Red Lake Indian Reservation any fish taken from the waters of Red Lake," but he informed all the fish companies that they would also "be liable to prosecution" if they bought Red Lake fish. The fisheries manager stationed in Redby, S. A. Selvog, was also indignant when he learned of the Red Lake Band's emerging plan for a legal test case, saying that the state "has certainly been fair to these people" by investing in the fishery facilities in Redby, building "one of the finest fish hatcheries in the state," and even making crushed ice readily available to the fisher men and women.[27]

The tribe's lawyer was not deterred, however, and decided to investigate whether federal treaties with tribes could resolve the issue of whether Red Lake fisher men and women might legally sell their fish off the reservation apart from the state business. The Indian agent for the BIA at Red Lake, Mark Burns, relayed his impression to the Game and Fish Commission in St. Paul that the people of Red Lake wanted the state out of their fishing economy and had a new strategy in mind for doing business. He wrote, "There seems to be a feeling prevalent among the Indians that the entire plant of the Minnesota State fisheries at Redby should be owned and operated by the Federal government instead of by the State of Minnesota and that it would be a very simple matter to procure an Act of Congress authorizing the use of tribal funds with which to purchase the buildings and equipment from the State and carry on the operation of the Fisheries plant and fish hatchery in the future."[28]

Not only did the Red Lake Ojibwe plan a legal test case in the fall of 1926, but some fisher men and women were already selling whitefish and walleye to a grocer in Red Lake Falls, a non-Indian town some distance from the reservation. When commissioner of Indian Affairs Charles H. Burke learned of Red Lake's challenge by engaging in selling their fish off the reservation, he responded with a more moderate view than the state of Minnesota. Burke expressed his opinion of Red Lake's proposed test case: "There is some merit in the belief of the Indians that they should have the right to sell or otherwise dispose of, outside the reservation, fish, game, hides, furs, etc., lawfully taken within the reservation. Therefore, if the Indians wish this question taken up in the state courts with a view of carrying it up for decision, this Office sees no objection to their doing so."[29]

Commissioner Gould would not back down and once again

asserted the state's authority over "commercial fishing in the waters of Red Lake." The continuing correspondence between St. Paul and Washington over Red Lake fishing included a recurring conversation about the legal consequences of extending citizenship to Indians. From Washington, Burke pointed out that citizenship did not "make the Indians on reservations subject to the laws of the state, it has been generally believed that the act did not have that effect either as to general criminal jurisdiction or as to the question of enforcement of state game and fish laws." At Red Lake, the fishing men and women continued to assert control over their labor and resources, and when a game warden from the Minnesota Department of Conservation visited the reservation community at Ponemah to investigate rumors that men and women there and at Battle River were using nets of the wrong size mesh, he was "given a fair warning not to touch or even come near their fishing equipment and informed . . . that he had no authority to come on the reservation for the purpose he was there or any other." Further, residents reveled in a bureaucratic rebuttal to the game warden when they suggested he should obtain for them written permission from the commissioner of Game and Fish to come onto the reservation in the first place.[30]

Agent Burns of Red Lake wrote to Washington to transmit the "proceedings of the General Council of the Red Lake Indians at a meeting held at Red Lake on February 5, 1927," when the council had expressed "considerable dissatisfaction" with "the price paid to the Indians by the state fisheries." Burns asked that Washington take up the issue with Minnesota's Game and Fish Commission.

In addition to still being unallotted in 1927, Red Lake had remarkably maintained structures of traditional governance. Long before the United States existed, Ojibwe people had a system of interconnected family groups with ties to an ancestral doodem which had organized family and community life for generations. This tradition allowed for a system of hereditary chiefs for community governance that operated alongside other legal structures to organize labor over ricing and fishing and other important economic activities. The Ojibwe relied on an Indigenous concept of doodem to explain their relationships, and through kinship networks they organized their political and social worlds. From the doodem they derived their sense of "nation."

The General Council at Red Lake evolved during the new era of commercial fishing and World War I, as the tribe adopted a written constitution in 1918. The General Council continued to place authority with the hereditary chiefs on the reservation, who each had the power to appoint to the council five members from their band or community and to call formal meetings. Red Lake's first tribal constitution committee was composed of five members, including Peter Graves, Otto Thunder, P. H. Beaulieau, and Joseph Graves. The document they produced combined aspects of Ojibwe governance and American constitutionalism. In addition, it was essential for Red Lake's General Council to declare a separate and sovereign political status, apart from the other Minnesota Ojibwe who were rapidly being dispossessed of their land.[31]

Peter Graves was also concerned with the legality of the fish royalties deducted from individual fisher men and women and paid to the greater tribe, and he questioned whether the state of Minnesota was able to enter into a contract arrangement with the band, citing federal law. In addition, in writing to Red Lake's lawyer in Walker, Graves cast doubt on the feasibility of the plan for defending a Red Lake Indian selling fish off the reservation as a test case.[32]

The state fishery on the Red Lake Reservation continued to produce controversy at Red Lake and within Minnesota, as legislators in St. Paul debated whether to allow fish to be sold beyond the state and whether to abolish the commercial fishing business entirely. Pressure came from fish companies in Minnesota and their attorneys, who argued that if fish at Red Lake were not limited to the wholesale trade, they would ask for an injunction to put an end to commercial fishing on the reservation. While the

Peter Graves, Red Lake tribal leader, 1953.

injunction eventually failed in the summer of 1927, commercial fishing continued for a short while under state management, at a time when the federal government was still pondering the future of the Red Lake Reservation—of the land and water, not just the fish.[33]

Commissioner Gould from Minnesota had inquired in Washington about a possible allotment of the Red Lake Reservation and what it might mean for future commercial fishing on Upper and Lower Red Lake. Commissioner Gould wanted to know not merely if Congress had plans to allot Red Lake but if it was contemplating other proposals for what was an exceptionally scenic landscape. He asked about a popular rumor in Minnesota that the federal government planned to appropriate the reservation land along the lake for a national park, which was not so unlikely a concept considering the recent annexation of large portions of the Leech Lake Reservation for the Chippewa National Forest. Commissioner Burke replied that while allotment was still planned for Red Lake and he expected Congress to soon authorize an appropriation to survey the reservation, "No definite proposition for setting aside a half mile strip of the shore line around Upper and Lower Red lake by the Federal Government as a national park has come before this office for consideration." Nonetheless, allotment would proceed, wrote Burke:

> The question of allotting the lands in severalty on the Red lake Indian Reservation has been thoroughly considered and the Superintendent has been authorized to advise the Indians that allotments will be made at as early a date as possible . . . The correspondence shows that there are 1712 Indians eligible to receive allotments and estimate that each eligible should receive the maximum area of 160 acres, the total allotted area would be 273,920 acres. There will still remain approximately 200,000 acres of tribal land after the Indians now eligible are allotted. As to whether any part of such tribal land lying outside the Red Lake Indian Forest Reserve shall be made available for sale under the settlement and entry plan, is a proposition that has not yet come before us for determination.[34]

Commissioner Gould had plenty of legal questions about Red Lake people and their land and resources, but he was reminded by Washington that even allotment in severalty would not "make the Indians subject to the fish and game laws of the state." At Red Lake, the General Council and fisher men and women continued to complain to their agent. They were dissatisfied with Commissioner Gould's oversight and believed the state unnecessarily delayed the opening of the fishing season. However, their greatest complaint was reserved for the extremely low prices paid them by the state for their fish, even after the fishery was finally allowed to market fish outside of Minnesota. As Agent Burns had reported might happen the year before, the General Council proposed instead that Washington use their tribal funds to purchase the fisheries plant on their reservation from Minnesota and operate it for the benefit of the band. Their proposal was supported by Congressman Harold Knutson of Minnesota's Sixth District, which included the Red Lake Reservation, and a small delegation from Red Lake—Joseph Jourdain, Roy Bailey, and Peter Graves—met with Minnesota governor Theodore Christianson and Commissioner Gould on February 19, 1927.[35]

The proposal by Graves and the Red Lake delegation was well thought out, and they suggested to the governor and commissioner that Section 5606 of the state's game and fish laws be amended in the interim so the state might continue to sell their fish inside or outside of Minnesota, though "at the highest price obtainable." They also lobbied senators and representatives from northern Minnesota about the management shift when they were in St. Paul. Even their competitors in the fish business were satisfied with the transfer to Washington if the Red Lake fishery planned to sell their fish at market prices. After a dozen years of

Filleting walleye at the fishery, about 1935.

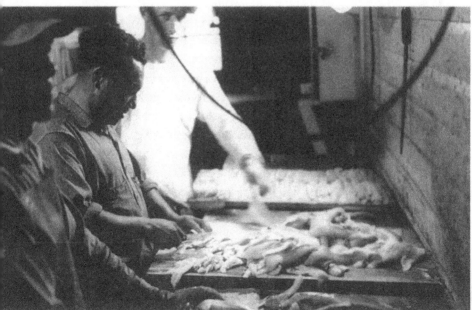

state management, on February 15, 1929, a bill was introduced in the Minnesota legislature to clear up the Red Lake fishing situation by authorizing the leasing of the state fisheries plant at Redby to the United States.[36]

The era of state management of a fishery on the Red Lake Reservation ended with opposition from more than one direction. Tribal fisher men and women desired more control over their day-to-day labor as well as the management of their commercial fishing business, and the state of Minnesota was plagued by complaints from fish wholesalers who opposed the state fishery on the reservation. In the waning days of state management, the district court of Ramsey County signed an order restraining the state Game and Fish Department from further engagement in the commercial purchase of fish at Red Lake after an injunction was filed against the state Game and Fish commissioner by a wholesale dealer. According to the state, Red Lake members did have a legal right to fish in 1929, and even to market their catch—but those who attempted to *purchase* Red Lake fish would find themselves in illegal possession of fish.[37]

The Red Lake Fisheries Association

The Ojibwe fisher men and women and the General Council that emerged on the reservation during the era of World War I made a number of strategic decisions about their labor when fishing became, almost overnight, a commercial enterprise that eventually connected them to markets as far away as Minneapolis, Chicago, and New York. Band members' profound cultural heritage and deep knowledge about fishing at Red Lake, which remains strong through the present day, was bound to conflict with an outside manager in the early years of commercial fishing, especially one with the rigid style of dealing with Indian tribes that characterized the Minnesota Department of Conservation. Although the fishery was developed to benefit non-Indian consumers, there

Mrs. Frank Gurneau and her mother dry nets, 1932.

were also helpful lessons from the first dozen years, as the state
brought the tribe into the arena of commercial fishing.

As the Minnesota legislature, the governor, and the courts
contemplated the future of Red Lake fishing during the winter of
1929, the Red Lake General Council and tribal members took action to ensure there would be a fishing season the following summer. The accomplished law firm of Dennis and Bell of Detroit
Lakes, hired to represent the tribe in the spring of 1927, entered
the world of federal Indian law with great energy and would work
with the tribe for many years to come. The tribe's lawyers understood the economic importance of fishing, writing in 1929 to the
state, "There is absolutely nothing that will promote the welfare
of 1800 people of Minnesota so much as the successful operation

of the Red Lake fisheries." For the moment, however, there was a legal problem to contend with, and the Red Lake agent Burns, attorney Fred Bell, and Peter Graves all landed in St. Paul to avert the possible crisis for the coming season. A businessman from Chicago who sold fishing supplies on the reservation wrote to Agent Burns summarizing the dilemma: "Thank you very much for your letter of January 25 and the situation with regards to Red Lake fish is both interesting and amusing. That is, the fact that the Indians have a right to catch the fish, but cannot sell them."[38]

On behalf of the Red Lake Band, Dennis and Bell entreated the commissioner of Fish and Game, by this time George W. McCullough, to see that the fisheries be continued "under the supervision of the state, the United States, or an association of the Indians" and asked for support in legislating the continuation of their industry. They sent the same message to the commissioner of Indian Affairs and notified him of an important tribal council to be held at Red Lake to discuss the future of the fishery. On March 1, 1929, the band's General Council established the Red Lake Fisheries Association, named the incumbent as its choice for a manager, and called for a higher tariff on fish imported from Canada.[39]

The Proceedings of the General Council of The Red Lake Band of Chippewa Indians meeting of March 1, 1929

Pursuant to the notice for the Red Lake Indian Council to meet this, the 1st day of March 1929, Joseph B. Jourdain, Chairman of the Council called the Council to order at 2:00 O'Clock p.m. and the following resolutions were adopted.

Resolution #1

WHEREAS the State of Minnesota, under the law as recently declared by decisions of the courts, cannot continue the operation of the Red Lake fisheries as it has in the past and it is necessary to provide a medium for handling the receipts and disbursements of said business: and,

WHEREAS, it is proposed to organize and incorporate the
Red Lake Indians who are engaged in the fishing industry
into an association under the laws of the State of Minnesota
with a board of directors, President, Vice-President, and
Secretary-treasurer to join with the State in the management
of the business:

THEREFORE be it resolved that the Indians engaged in fishing in the waters of the Red Lake Reservation organize and
incorporate as an association to be called "Red Lake Fisheries
Association" and that a board of directors of five (5) members
at this time be selected, and that said board be authorized
to elect from its members a President, Vice-President, and
Secretary-treasurer, that the business in the future be conducted under joint management of the State of Minnesota and
said association, and that the association and the members
thereof comply with the rules and regulations prescribed by
the Commissioner of Game and Fish of the State of Minnesota,
provided such rules and regulation do not infringe or conflict
with the laws of the United States or such rules and regulations
as may be prescribed by the Secretary of the Interior or the
Commissioner of Indian Affairs.

The above resolution was adopted by the Council and pursuant
there John Wind, Simon Stately, Peter Sitting, Peter Graves and
Benjamin Littlecreek were duly elected members of the first
board of directors of the proposed association.

Resolution # 2

WHEREAS, it is necessary that the Red Lake fisheries in the future be under the joint management of the State of Minnesota
and the Red Lake Indians: and,

WHEREAS, Honorable George W. McCullough has offered to
select as manager and place in charge of the business for the
State Mr. A. C. Klancke, who has been connected with the
State Game & Fish Department for many years:

THEREFORE be it resolved that the offer of the State Game
& Fish Commissioner in this connection be approved and
accepted, and that the Commissioner be requested to authorize
Mr. A. C. Klancke to cooperate with the Red Lake fisheries
association in conducting the Red Lake fisheries.

The resolution was adopted.

Resolution #3

WHEREAS large quantities of fish are imported into the United
States from the Dominion of Canada annually, thus coming
into competition with fish and fish products produced in the
United States: and,

WHEREAS the Red Lake Indians of the Red Lake reservation
in Minnesota produce fish of the market value of $100,000.00
annually which must be sold in competition with the fish
imported from the Dominion of Canada and which greatly
limits the market and reduces the price obtainable for the fish
produced from the waters of the Red Lake reservation;

THEREFORE be it resolved that the Commissioner of Indian
Affairs, and that the United States Senators, and Congress-
men from the State of Minnesota and the Congress of the
United States, be importuned to use their influence to secure
legislation providing for a higher protective tariff on fish and
fish products imported into the United States from foreign
countries.

The resolution was adopted.

We, the undersigned, Joseph B. Jourdain, Chairman, and Peter
Graves, Secretary, of the Red Lake Council, do hereby certify
that the following named Councilmen were present at this
meeting, which adjourned at 6 O'Clock p.m. March 1st, 1929,
VIZ:

Okemahwahjewabe,	Ahjedumo,
Waymetigoshwwahcumig,	William Sayers,
Mesahbay,	Simon Spears,
Mayskogwon,	Joe Mason,
Kaykezhegwonabe,	Keniew Sumner,
Omahyahwegabow,	Peter Clark,
Edward Holeinday,	Wayzowegwonabe,
John Wind,	Aindussoonding,
Spencer Whitefeather,	Teddy Rosebear,
George Spears,	Charley Rosebear,
Blake Rosebear,	Tom Stillday,
Sam Blackcrow,	John George,
Ahshubishkahwenenee,	Mike French,
Jack Rush,	Alvin Burns,
Harry Johnson,	William Jourdain,
Kecheahibay,	Louis Stately,
Ke we tah be nais,	Robert Rain,
Charley Jourdain,	Peter Graves,
Kebedwayosay,	Miskokeniew,
Solomon Blue,	Way Jaun,
Chas. A. Beaulieu,	Zozay Boxer.

We further certify, that we have caused, on this the 5th day of March, 1929, to be delivered the original and one copy of these proceedings to Mr. Mark L. Burns, Superintendent, the original for transmittal to the Commissioner of Indian Affairs.

Joseph B. Jourdain.
Chairman.

Peter Graves.
Secretary.

Redlake, Minn.
March 1, 1929.[40]

In a historic moment for the tribe and for commercial fishing at Red Lake, the Ojibwe fishing men and women formally organized a corporation, one with a board of directors and officers, in order to "join with the State in the management of the business." After March 1, 1929, the Red Lake Fisheries Association elected officers and met regularly. By March 25, the new agreement had passed both branches of the Minnesota legislature and been signed by the governor. The tribe and the state became joint managers of commercial fishing at Red Lake, allowing the upcoming fishing season to proceed. Commissioner of Indian Affairs Burke weighed in from Washington, advising Agent Burns at Red Lake that, "as all the Indians are entitled to fish," there was no longer a need for permits. Letters began to flow into the reservation from businesses asking to purchase fish, including a restaurant in Walker, Minnesota, that wished to immediately be informed if it would soon "be able to serve wall-eyed pike."[41]

An agreement was negotiated to pay salaries for a small number of fisheries employees, including a foreman and a bookkeeper, and a lease was drawn up between the Red Lake Fisheries Association and the commissioner of Game and Fish for Minnesota for the actual fisheries plant in Redby. The state fishery on the reservation had been a profitable business; a surplus of funds sat in the state treasury at the time of the new agreement with the state of Minnesota. The tribe's lawyers made a cogent argument: "The whole property at Redby has been paid for out of funds acquired from the enterprise. Furthermore, a substantial fund has been built up in the state treasury so it would not seem fair to require the Association to pay an upkeep on the plant unless the sum actually is expended for that purpose."[42]

The tribe's lawyers pointed to the logic that since the fund in the state treasury derived from Red Lake fishing, it should therefore support the work of the fishery, including the hatchery. Then the Red Lake "Indians will receive the benefit of the fund that they really have produced."[43]

The good feelings were not to last. In the 1930s, the state proved to be a tightfisted and duplicitous partner. In 1938, Fred Dennis wrote a frank letter to Herman Wenzel, commissioner of conservation, outlining the terms under which the Red Lake Fisheries Association might "continue to function as a business," which included reducing costs to the association.

The next year, Dennis wrote a heated letter to Governor Harold Stassen questioning the state's activities in the contested region of Upper Red Lake. In 1935, using $15,000 from the state fish fund, the state had purchased land near the Tamarac River as well as buildings in the village of Waskish. The Red Lake Band, consistently asserting those lands to be rightfully part of the reservation, had hoped to have the land and water on the east side of Upper Red Lake surrounding Waskish returned to them, but the state was now using funds from the association's own fishing revenue in ways that worked against not only the fisher men and women's interests but those of the entire band.

At that point [in Upper Red Lake] is the village of Waskish, and besides buying the land referred to the State bought every building of every nature in the village, and stated as a reason for so doing that it was for the quarters of the employees of the fish hatchery, if and when one was built.

I can inform you that upon examination of the buildings in that village I could not find one that had ever seen any paint; and it would be unreasonable, to my mind at least, for the State to ever make any use of them.

The State of Minnesota actually paid $10,754.09 in these condemnation proceedings for buying this property. This money was originally a part of the State Fish Revolving fund, which was an accumulation of the profits made by the State of Minnesota prior to 1929 when it was operating the fisheries business at Redby. The money practically all came out of the profits from the sale of fish produced in Red Lake, within the boundaries of the Red Lake Indian Reservation.

> In my opinion it was the most extravagant, wanton,
> and uncalled for expenditure of funds of the State that
> could have been made and the purchase of the property
> was unwarranted and needless and it will never be of any
> value whatsoever to our State.[44]

Dennis sent copies of his letter to Beltrami and Becker County representatives and also to the commissioner of Indian Affairs in Washington, DC. In other letters to Washington, Dennis expressed his view that the land sale and other purchases were "caused by some feeling in opposition to the Indians of Minnesota and particularly the Red Lake Band."[45]

The Red Lake agent, Raymond H. Bitney, agreed with the tribe's lawyer about restoring the missing portions of Upper Red Lake, calling for the tribe's exclusive management of the entire lake as well as a sensible resolution to issues involving the reservation fishery. Pointing out that the fishery buildings at Redby were constructed during wartime and years when the state of Minnesota supervised the fishing, he wrote to tribal leader Peter Graves:

> I have been wondering if this is not a very opportune
> time for the Indians to request that the State of Minnesota
> grant to them that portion of Red Lake in the northern
> end of it which was taken away from them in the Treaty
> of 1889 and should be restored to them, and in addition
> to that portion of Upper Red Lake which is not inside the
> shore of the lake be given to the Indians and become part
> of their reservation. In addition to the exclusive control of
> the lake and the restoration of the lake to the reservation,
> it would be well to ask the State of Minnesota to turn over
> to the Red Lake Cooperative Fisheries Association or to
> the Red Lake tribe the fisheries building, fisheries lease,
> and the hatchery at Redby, with all the appurtenances
> and equipment and the assignment of the lease on the

Red Lake townsite to the Red Lake Fisheries Association
or the Red Lake tribe. This should clear up for all time
the present squabble that is going on between the State of
Minnesota Conservation Department and the Red Lake
Band of Chippewas.[46]

Bitney's advocacy for the rights of Red Lake people reflected
the new direction of Indian policy from Washington, which
throughout the 1930s called for greater economic and political autonomy. The Red Lake Fisheries Association, formed on the eve
of a major political change in Washington, was exactly the kind
of economic enterprise the Bureau of Indian Affairs now desired
for Indian Country. Back in Minnesota, the working relationship
between the state and the Red Lake Ojibwe, even after formation
of the Red Lake Fisheries Association, continued to be strained
by racism and tainted by state corruption. When the annual contract was up for renegotiation in 1939, Peter Graves, a member of
the association as well as secretary of the General Council, wrote
an unflinchingly defiant letter to Harry E. Speakes of the Game
and Fish Department outlining Minnesota's exploitation of the
tribe and its fishery:

> Your department has been suggesting expense and chang-
> ing of fishing methods so that it would be impossible for
> this association to continue operation. So far as I am per-
> sonally concerned you may come and take your buildings
> which we are occupying at any time you so desire. The
> state of Minnesota owns the buildings acquired by unlaw-
> ful methods, as I understand, as found by its own court,
> of which you must be aware. These buildings were built
> from profits of the Red Lake Fisheries, most of the money
> being earned by the Red Lake Indians as not one penny
> of Minnesota taxpayers money went into these buildings.
> If I am wrong in this matter you might ask your advisor,
> Mr. George Weaver, Superintendent of Commercial

Fishing, who has never been friendly to the interests of
the Red Lake Indian fishermen, and who, I understand, is
back of the move to attempt to change the method of fishing on Red Lake and who has spread exaggerated reports
of the waste in fish on Red Lake. It appears that as long
as you are dealing with an inferior race of people there
should be no consideration given regardless of conditions.

You may come and take over your buildings just as
soon as you please since showing your attitude, but I hope
you do not write me any more letters of the nature you
have written as you do not need to quote law or anything
else, as the record of your department speaks for itself
insofar as the interest of the Red Lake Fisheries Association is concerned. The Governor is not very far from your
office. You might call and talk with him on this matter
without prejudice.[47]

The tribe's lawyer, having read a carbon copy, expressed with
some admiration, "Wow! I burned my fingers turning over the
first page."[48]

The fishery buildings were finally transferred from the state
to the United States and have been held in trust for the tribe
since 1943. The minutes of the Red Lake Fisheries Association's
annual meetings show productive members from across the reservation, many of whom were women. At the peak of its early
twentieth-century membership, approximately 240 Red Lake
Ojibwe men and women were working and voting members of
the association, and because the labor of fishing was shared by so
many relatives, even with the arrival of commercial fishing, any
income paid to the membership benefitted a significant portion
of the reservation population. The Red Lake Nation still operates
a commercial fishery at Redby, the oldest walleye fishery in the
United States, though in the present day their greatest concern
is for protecting the lake's water quality and its resources from
overharvesting and decline. Today members of a new genera-

tion, the descendants of those men and women who formed the Red Lake Fisheries Association, persist in their spiritual and legal commitment toward the restoration of the missing portions of the upper lake.[49]

Naynaabeak and the Game Warden

In 1939, an Ojibwe man named Max Jones sent a courteous letter to the superintendent of the Red Lake Indian Reservation about his mother, Naynaabeak, or Anna Jones. The Jones family lived near the Canadian border, on allotments of land located a short distance from the northern edge of the reservation. Mr. Jones's letter was one of complaint, yet he patiently explained to the reservation superintendent that a state game warden was "dragging the river" for logging use along the banks past his mother's allotment, making it impossible for her to set a net for fishing. Max Jones wrote in the spring, "Mother, Mrs. Anna Jones or Nay-Na-A-Beak, wishes to get a permit if possible, so she can put her small net in the Warroad River where her land joins, alongside of her house. The Game Warden drags through there all the time which is impossible to maintain fishing grounds. If you can possibly send her a permit, so she can have a right to fish there, we will appreciate it very much."[50]

This ordinary letter, like countless others received by Indian agencies, similar in subject to scores of letters Indian people wrote about their working lives, introduces some of the complexities that American Indian men, women, and families experienced in early twentieth-century Minnesota. The Jones family lived within an Indigenous community in Warroad, Minnesota, a town that bordered not only an Indian reservation but also the United States and Canada. They were Ojibwe people and tribal citizens enrolled at Red Lake, but they lived on an allotment of land rather than on a reservation. Most significantly, Naynaabeak's home and fishing spot was historically an Ojibwe place—Anishinaabewaki or a homeland. Born around 1875,

Naynaabeak lived her days among French settlers and newer Scandinavian immigrants who were loggers and farmers, as well as her own relatives and people. The Jones family inhabited a complex legal world increasingly defined by borders that disrupted their ability to make a living, so that by Naynaabeak's time, a conflict with a game warden was simply part of day-to-day existence for Ojibwe people. Fortunately, the issue was soon resolved after the superintendent's intervention.

Naynaabeak had a relationship to that river where she set her net and worked, as did her ancestors, and possibly as do even her descendants today, since Ojibwe people still fish the Warroad River, one of the tributaries of the Lake of the Woods. Lake of the Woods is one of many Ojibwe landscapes in the Great Lakes and upper Mississippi region that has held the Anishinaabeg in place for many generations, landscapes where women maintained not only legal rights but a spiritual and economic responsibility for water. At the same time, it was a characteristic of Ojibwe philosophy and world views to place greater emphasis on their *responsibilities* to the land, water, and its resources, rather than simply on their *right* to exploit them. Women fished, in addition to harvesting wild rice from the headwaters of rivers and from lakes, and organized their labor collectively and in ways that demonstrated excellent management of the natural environment. Through these essential activities they considered themselves to be stewards of the water, taking responsibility for caring for its resources. In Ojibwe culture, water was a gendered space where women possessed property rights, which they demonstrated through their long-standing practice of binding rice together into sheaves prior to harvest, part of an Indigenous legal system that marked territory on a lake and empowered women. From every legal angle that mattered to Ojibwe women, and in consideration of the need to make a living, Naynaabeak was obliged to set her fishing net in the Warroad River, despite the difficulties she faced in doing so by 1939.[51]

Naynaabeak's way of life was not so different from that of many other American Indian men and women who survived on reservations or allotments of land in the early twentieth century, and who by letter or action, such as setting a small fishing net, continued to exercise their right to work and earn a living. That they frequently carried out these activities on Indigenous homelands, whether in Minnesota or other areas of the United States, presented a continuous challenge to the political and legal structures that came to define the reservation and post-allotment era. Naynaabeak and her generation faced enormous hurdles in their determination to make a living, and the people rarely became prosperous, but their efforts to survive and remain on their lands, fishing grounds, forests, hills, and mountains—and especially their sacred places—allowed their descendants to maintain Indigenous communities that exist to the present day.

4

Jingle Dress Dancers in the Modern World

The Influenza of 1918–19

When I was growing up, my grandmother, Jeanette Auginash, wore a jingle dress at powwows on the Red Lake Reservation, especially during our mid-summer gathering, which was then associated with a Fourth of July celebration. During the assimilation years, American Indian people often persuaded Indian agents and federal officials to view their powwows as events held to show their respect for the United States, but this was really only a clever ploy to continue holding traditional gatherings in an era when such activities were being banned and suppressed. Nevertheless, most Red Lake people have extremely fond memories of the annual Fourth of July powwow and celebration, which for us had little to do with patriotism, aside from the small parade of veterans who carried flags into and out of the arena. In those days, holding the powwow on July 4 not only became a tradition in its own right but was convenient for family members who lived off the reservation since their jobs allowed them vacation to return home.[1]

In the years before the contest powwow revolutionized decades of convention, more people from the community danced, and Ojibwe women often hastily sewed their own jingle dresses together in the weeks and days prior to July 4. Back then, jingle dresses were far simpler than the finery of today's regalia. I remember Jeanette's dresses as being rather simple, a sheath of plain black cotton, perhaps with sequins and a single row of jingles near the hem. When I was a child in the 1960s and '70s, jingle dresses were worn exclusively by elderly women, rarely by younger women or girls. I had no idea of the origin of the Ojibwe jingle dress or its songs and dances. It was clear that female elders deeply valued them, but all I knew was that Jeanette strongly identified with the tradition, and to my mind it was therefore "old." I never thought to ask my grandmother about her plain black jingle dress, and I never imagined it might be related to anything that existed beyond our own Ojibwe communities.

As scholars have noted, epidemic diseases were devastatingly critical events for American Indians, yet the historical record about them seems to have produced little more than "native silence, if not total amnesia, surrounding these horrendous events." The Ojibwe Jingle Dress Dance is a firm counterargument to the notion that American Indians have been silent about the role of epidemics in their history, since the dress, dance, songs, and associated stories are steeped in historical narratives about a terrible epidemic. And since the tradition emerged during World War I, an extensive body of evidence, including oral histories, photographs, material culture, and documents, links the jingle dress to the global influenza epidemic that killed millions of people worldwide, including thousands of North American Indians and Alaska Natives.[2]

The decade of the epidemic was the only one of the twentieth century when the Red Lake Ojibwe population declined. The pandemic probably started in rural Kansas, and it soon spread in three waves, in the spring and fall of 1918 and the winter of 1919, to remote reservations in addition to more populated towns and metropolitan areas. Inexplicably, despite the loss of 675,000 American lives, the epidemic is not widely known or remembered in the United States. For Ojibwe women, though, the epidemic also had an effect on Ojibwe culture and traditions of work that are observable even today, especially women's approaches to healing.[3]

The Ojibwe women who experienced and survived the terrible epidemic were the first to recognize the therapeutic power of the jingle dress, and they infused a modern disaster with uniquely

Red Lake men, women, and children, 1920s.

Indigenous cultural symbols of healing as they worked in their communities throughout the crisis. The Jingle Dress Dance was a revolutionary new tradition of healing that appears to have surfaced simultaneously in Ojibwe communities of both the United States and Canada. Women invented new performative rituals as they worked to restore health to those stricken by influenza, at the same time delivering spiritual sustenance to others who lost relatives and loved ones to the deadly disease. Likewise, a number of Ojibwe women risked their own health by selflessly laboring as nurses for the duration as the demand for a volunteer work force swiftly emerged to cope with the sickness and the astonishing death toll of the epidemic. On reservations and in cities, on pow-wow grounds and in hospital wards, the modern labor history of Ojibwe women was shaped, renewed, and ultimately transformed by the first global pandemic of the twentieth century.[4]

Later in the century, the influenza all but forgotten, the Ojibwe Jingle Dress Dance underwent a remarkable, pan-tribal revival. Today most American Indians, and certainly the women from tribes across North America who perform the dance and wear jingle dresses, in addition to men who compose and sing the songs associated with it as part of drum groups, continue to attach great importance to its longer association with healing, though a younger generation may not recall its Ojibwe origins or have ever heard of the epidemic.

Ojibwe people associate the jingle dress with therapeutic rituals that support physical healing, but spiritual and emotional healing constitutes another essential purpose. In every part of community and economic life related to the well-being of families and health, Ojibwe women were especially active, and the jingle dress and rituals associated with it are part of their legacy. Women demonstrated an extraordinary commitment to good life and health, even during the post-allotment turmoil in the Great Lakes, through continued dedication to ceremonial life, Indigenous forms of healing, and perhaps most dynamically as laborers in the traditional economy. Taken as a whole, Ojibwe women formidably counteracted the strain of negative influences associated with the forces of settler colonialism that emerged with reservation life.

Ojibwe women engaged their changing world straight on. They adapted gender roles and expectations and adjusted labor practices to the new circumstances of the reservation. Women, as well as men, worked as healers within their communities and practiced what today we call holistic medicine. Their vocation allowed the most proficient individuals to identify and gather plants for everyday and occasional use for a range of conditions. Women continued to harvest food, just as they had in the pre-reservation era. Wild rice and maple syrup are examples of the bounty of women's labor. Women worked as the principal harvesters of wild rice, bringing good health and stability to

Ojibwe life in years otherwise notable for land loss, deprivation, and crisis.

The Origin of the Jingle Dress Dance

Historians often fail to appreciate the historical circumstances that gave rise to aspects of American Indian cultural life, and song and dance are perhaps especially enigmatic. Too often, we erroneously view Indigenous institutions, including practices arising in the twentieth century, as part of a mysterious and time-less past. In fact, Ojibwe storytelling frequently refers to specific times, places, relationships, and events. For example, it is often recalled in public storytelling at Red Lake that a visiting drum group from Fort Berthold in North Dakota gave a flag song to the community during World War II, and since then the same song prefaces formal gatherings on the reservation. Fort Berthold is a Mandan, Hidatsa, and Arikara community, but with strong ties to the Ojibwe people of Red Lake in the twentieth century. Whenever the flag song is performed, Ojibwe people on the reservation recall a period when men left to serve in Europe, the Pacific, and North Africa and a number of women and families departed their small communities to find work in the cities. A drum group performing the flag song allows the community to remember a moment of great change at Red Lake, when events of the larger world became part of our tribal narratives. The performance of the flag song, especially in the presence of visitors or a drum group from Fort Berthold, also honors and renews bonds between the reservation communities and recognizes that shared experience of the war.[5]

The Jingle Dress Dance also has a modern story carrying a powerful history. It flourished under extraordinarily harsh conditions in the Great Lakes. Not only was 1918–19 a time of global warfare and disease, but Ojibwe communities were experiencing a second wave of dispossession and economic decline following the allotment of their reservations. State and local governments joined with timber company interests, reducing Native title and ownership on all reservations, and particularly at White Earth.

The following story about the origin of the Jingle Dress Dance is the one I learned at Red Lake. An Ojibwe girl became very sick. She appeared to be near death. Her father, fearing the worst, sought a vision to save her life, and this was how he learned of a unique dress and dance. The father made this dress for his daughter and asked her to dance a few springlike steps, in which one foot was never to leave the ground. Before long, she felt stronger and kept up the dance. After her recovery, she continued to dance in the special dress, and eventually she formed the first Jingle Dress Dance Society.[6]

The setting for the story is sometimes given as the Mille Lacs Ojibwe community in north-central Minnesota, sometimes as Whitefish Bay in northwestern Ontario. Both communities, while separated by hundreds of miles, express a great devotion to Anishinaabe traditions of song and dance. A specific young girl is identified as the first jingle dress dancer, though she has a different name in each community. The story suggests an influenza-like illness, making it plausible that the first jingle dress dancer suffered from the widespread epidemic of Spanish Influenza during the time of World War I.

The Jingle Dress Dance was dream-given to the Ojibwe people. Although a man conceived the Jingle Dress Dance after receiving a vision, women were responsible for its proliferation. It was not unusual for a man who had experienced a particularly strong vision to share it with other people, and sometimes with the community at large. Once the influenza epidemic struck, women applied the ceremony like a salve to fresh wounds. They designed jingle dresses, organized sodalities, and danced at tribal gatherings large and intimate, spreading a new tradition while participating in innovative rituals of healing. Special healing songs are associated with the jingle dress, and both songs and dresses possess a strong therapeutic value. Women who participate in the Jingle Dress Dance and wear these special dresses do so to ensure the health and well-being of an individual, a family, or even the broader tribal community.[7]

Federal Policy and the Freedom to Dance

The jingle dress tradition coincided with a new round of Indian religion being suppressed in the United States, as the Dance Order from Washington arrived in 1921. As historian John Troutman has established in his creative and original study, *Indian Blues: American Indians and the Politics of Music, 1879–1934,* "up until the late 1920s, the office of Indian Affairs (OIA) had spent decades waging vigorous opposition to dances on reservations and continually sought new ways to suppress them by practically any means available." There is little doubt that Ojibwe women disregarded the new ruling because historical photographs show them in jingle dresses dating from roughly 1920 and every decade thereafter, first on reservations and later in the cities. When the jingle dress was introduced it was an innovation, but one consistent with Ojibwe spiritual practices and traditions of song and dance. Troutman's research shows that despite the repression and surveillance that characterized reservation life, as assimilation policies were pressed forward by agents and other federal employees, not to mention their allies in Christian organizations, "Native people constantly innovated and expanded their repertoires of expressive culture in ways that both reflected their experiences and transformed their circumstances."[8]

The Jingle Dress Dance was also an Indigenous, anti-colonial movement because the new social practice came into being, was organized, and flourished under the Indian office ban on ritualistic dance. Neither the promise of citizenship nor the potential for reprimand discouraged Indian dance, which thrived on the reservation. As federal policy continued in the senseless direction of dismantling tribalism in the early decades of the twentieth century, for the Ojibwe the Jingle Dress Dance no doubt "served as a vehicle of freedom through which they expressed an increased sense of autonomy over segments of their own lives," to apply Troutman's view of an expanding expressive culture on reservations. Like their Lakota neighbors on the plains, the Ojibwe did not curtail their traditions of dance as they lived under the observation of Indian agents and missionaries but, contrary to expectations, they "succeeded in vastly expanding their dance traditions."[9]

The Jingle Dress Dance spread rapidly throughout Ojibwe Country and soon reached the Ojibwe's Dakota neighbors, following the patterns of early trade routes established in the Great Lakes and upper Midwest. Dakota women added their own artistic flourishes and social processes. Dakota communities such as Spirit Lake (Fort Totten) in North Dakota, whose members maintain enduring ties of friendship and culture to the Ojibwe at Red Lake, have taken great pride in their Jingle Dress Dance tradition. For several generations now, Dakota women have also designed, sewn, and worn jingle dresses at powwows, at Red Lake and in their own communities. The Dance Order from Washington had no control or influence over the popularity and diffusion of the Jingle Dress Dance throughout the Great Lakes and upper Midwest.[10]

The Making of a Jingle Dress

Jingle dress dancing holds a spiritual power for Indian people because of its association with healing. In the world of the Ojibwe, spiritual power moves through air. Sounds hold significance. The jingle dress is special because of the rows of metal cones, ziibaaska'iganan in Ojibwemowin, that dangle from the garment's fabric to produce a pleasantly dissonant rattle as they bounce against one another. The effect is greater when many women dance together. When jingle dresses first appeared, they resembled women's ceremonial and popular dresses of the era, but the rows of jingles were new. Innovation is always a part of powwow and dance regalia, and the jingle dress is no exception, but dresses through the decades share many common features.[11]

A dress from the early twentieth century, held in the collections of the Minnesota Historical Society, was designed by Mary Bigwind of the White Earth Reservation and belonged to her granddaughter Madeline when she was a teenager. It is a sleeveless, black velvet dress with an empire waist. Single lines of jingles are sewn in neat rows at the bodice, hip, knee, and hemline. The jingles are fashioned from round snuff can lids pressed into the distinctive shape of a cone. Dancers often completed their ensemble with a belt. My grandmother Jeanette and older women at Red Lake wore rather simple jingle dresses at powwows.[12]

The use of a variety of shells, metals, coins, and jingles to adorn regalia has a long and well-documented history in the Great Lakes and upper Midwest. However, the use of metal cones to trim Indigenous regalia does not by itself make a garment a "jingle dress." Copper, tin, brass, silver, and the enormously popular lid of the Copenhagen snuff can, shaped into cones, have been used for the decoration of many objects of material culture, including bags, jewelry, cradleboards, drums, and men's shirts, in addition to women's dresses. Ojibwe people have a long history of wearing jingles, and they were photographed in jingles before 1920. One well-known image shows Bagone-giizhig wearing a necklace of spent ammunition casings.[13]

Jingle dress sewn by Mary Bigwind.

The visual history of the jingle dress in the Great Lakes, recorded in hundreds of images of Ojibwe women in early twentieth-century photographs and postcards from Wisconsin, Minnesota, and Ontario, confirms that the jingle dress emerged just prior to 1920, around the time of the influenza pandemic. Photographs on postcards can be dated fairly easily, not only by their postmarks but also by the formats used in their printing. In the case of postcards on which real photographs were printed, the style of stamp boxes on postcard backs changed at fairly regular intervals from 1900 to 1960. For example, postcards with an AZO stamp box where the arrows point upward were produced between 1915 and 1922, while those with AZO and squares at each corner appear from about 1921 to 1930. However, when dating postcards it is also important to bear in mind that popular photographic images of American Indian subjects were often printed on postcards long after the pictures were taken. As a result, other information may help to contextualize the picture and confirm the approximate date of its original making.[14]

The extensive photograph and visual database collections of the Minnesota Historical Society and Marquette University in Milwaukee, Wisconsin, indicate that women were not pictured in jingle dresses before 1920. The earliest Minnesota postcard showing a jingle dress comes from Pequot Lakes, about forty miles northwest of Mille Lacs, with a postmark of 1925 and an AZO square back. Over the next decade, postcards depicting Ojibwe women from Minnesota feature jingle dresses more than any other regalia. By 1930, jingle dresses are seen on postcards from all regions of Minnesota, including one postmarked Cass Lake in 1931 and another from Bena in 1940. By the 1930s, it is also possible to locate postcards of women from North Dakota attired in jingle dresses. Dakota women from Spirit Lake often acquired their dresses as gifts from special friends at Red Lake and White Earth. While it is clear that the Jingle Dress Dance tradition emerged soon after the influenza pandemic, and while Canadian Ojibwe communities were hit very hard by the flu, the earliest postcard

A group in regalia on the street at Pequot Lakes.

depicting a jingle dress from the Rainy Lake and Rainy River region of southwestern Ontario does not appear until later.[15]

The styles of early jingle dresses followed popular fashions of the day, with sailor collars and the loose, slim lines of 1920s flapper dresses, as in the one designed by Mary Bigwind. Jingle dresses in succeeding decades appear to be more tightly fitted, as were the dress styles of the 1940s. Over time, women enhanced the jingle dress with a variety of creative embellishments, including Ojibwe floral beadwork appliqué or pearl buttons. At mid-century, when women often added rows of jingles, dark colors and velvet cloth were popular.

Postcards provide visual evidence of the jingle dress's changing style through the decades but also maintain consistency with Ojibwe stories from Minnesota. The earliest and largest concentration of postcard pictures of Ojibwe women in jingle dresses appears in north-central Minnesota, the location of the Mille Lacs Reservation, between 1920 and 1925. On the whole, the visual evidence suggests that the one-piece jingle dress first emerged in Minnesota shortly after the influenza pandemic of 1918. Yet the Jingle Dress Dance, for all its importance and decades of popularity, seemed a tradition in sharp decline in the 1970s, when elderly women like my grandmother were the only dancers to be found wearing jingle dresses at powwows in Ojibwe Country.

The Diffusion of the Jingle Dress Dance

Anthropologists Patricia Albers and Beatrice Medicine witnessed the "sudden explosion and spread of jingle dresses and dancing" that took place on the powwow circuit in the 1980s. In fact, they cited the jingle dress trend as one reason it is challenging for scholars to write about the powwow, an "ever-changing and expanding world" with both "enormous changes" as well as "persisting traditions." In *Heartbeat of the People: Music and Dance of the Northern Pow-wow,* Tara Browner, an ethnomusicologist of Choctaw ancestry, wrote about her own experience as a jingle dress dancer on the powwow circuit for seven years and the reverence she has for the tradition:

> The very act of dancing in this dress constitutes a prayer
> for healing, and often spectators, musicians, and other
> dancers will make gifts of tobacco to a dancer and request
> that she pray for an ill family member while she dances.
> An example of hidden spirituality and ritual within a
> public forum, the ever-unfolding story of the Jingle Dress
> Dance is unique in Indian Country. There is little fanfare
> and no public announcement when the Jingle Dance is
> performed as a healing prayer, only a quiet circulation
> of family members from dancer to dancer, a whispered
> request, and a quick nod of thanks by both parties.[16]

A dance at Red Lake, about 1956.

Today scholars also view the Jingle Dress Dance tradition as an "ever-unfolding" movement in the "ever-changing" way American Indians create and adapt the powwow to new circumstances. As Albers and Medicine have explained, "songs, styles of singing and dancing, and regalia designs unique to particular tribes and regions are now crossing cultural boundaries more and more often." Many American Indian people appreciate the Jingle Dress Dance tradition as a "prayer of healing," and its widespread adoption by other tribal women, especially since the 1980s, suggests that people from all over Native North America find power and meaning in its ceremonial performance.[17]

The Indian Gaming and Regulatory Act of 1989, which has been credited with lifting some American Indian tribes out of poverty and stimulating economic growth in rural America, contributed to a prosperity that allowed for an expansion of the contest powwow throughout Indian Country. It also may have saved the Jingle Dress Dance tradition. Decades after a deadly epidemic ignited the new performative tradition on Ojibwe reservations, the Jingle Dress Dance suddenly began to flourish into a far broader pan-Indian phenomenon popular with Indian girls and women of all ages and tribal affiliations. From the Gathering of Nations in Albuquerque to the Mashantucket Pequot Powwow in Connecticut, the jingle dress became not only a popular form of regalia but a new category of female dance as the contest powwow was launched.

As it evolved, the Ojibwe Jingle Dress Dance maintained its integrity as a dance of healing. Although the health of American Indians has improved greatly, along with life expectancy, since World War II, there has been a rise in chronic disease in recent years, especially diabetes, often described as "epidemic" in the Southwest and northern plains since the 1980s. A new plague of chronic disease corresponds with the more recent spread of the Jingle Dress Dance in those regions of Indian Country. The jingle dress, a gift of healing from the Ojibwe people, has adapted and survived and continues to inspire American Indian women and their communities.[18]

Health and Healers on Early Twentieth-Century Ojibwe Reservations

By the time of the 1918 outbreak, tuberculosis had replaced smallpox as the largest health threat to Indians, and the number of TB patients on reservations, in boarding schools, and in sanatoriums multiplied. Trachoma was also pervasive. The highly contagious eye disease was not deadly, but it caused misery and suffering for otherwise healthy children and families. It first appeared in government boarding schools before afflicting the general Indian population in disproportionate numbers. Ojibwe women, perhaps more than ever, found their special healing knowledge in demand.[19]

Government physicians trivialized the medical expertise of Ojibwe women, though women persisted in their work. Doctors, confounded by the dismal state of health in Indian communities, blamed Indian families for creating unsanitary living conditions and contributing to high rates of tuberculosis and other diseases. They also asserted western ideas and approaches to the body, health, and disease. The Ojibwe method of health and wellness, which linked the physical body to spiritual and emotional health, came under attack in the reservation period, as critics charged that these beliefs held Indians back from assimilation and racial advance.

Dr. Thomas Rodwell, the physician for Red Lake in the early twentieth century, shared the outlook of his contemporaries in government service. Rodwell made no mention of women's work when he addressed the problem of tuberculosis and smallpox on the Red Lake Reservation in a narrative to Washington in 1906. But he made only sporadic visits to the Indian community, living closer to the agency in Walker, seventy-five miles away. Rodwell's reports reflected shortcomings characteristic of the profession of agency doctor, chief among them a limited experience with and a disdain for the medicinal and spiritual practices in the Indian community where he worked.[20]

Rodwell was pleased to discover that most members of the Red Lake community did not resist western medical interventions and were amenable to his services. Relentlessly pragmatic, Red Lake people accepted western medicine, adding it to their long-standing repertoire of Indigenous healing. Rodwell misinterpreted the willingness of Ojibwe people to visit the doctor as a sign of cultural submission. In a triumphant communication to his supervisors, he proclaimed a moral victory over traditional spiritual practices at Red Lake: "The Indians under my professional charge have now almost entirely given up their grand medicine ideas and are availing themselves of the professional services and remedies of the Agency physician."[21]

Although Rodwell never imagined as fellow medical practitioners the Ojibwe women who worked with plants and medicines beyond his gaze, he could see the utility of Euroamerican field matrons. He requested that Washington assign recruits to northern Minnesota, confident that field matrons might be "of very great comfort and welfare to the women and children and the sick." Five years later, a staff of field matrons worked among the Ojibwe in Minnesota. One was Josephine Bonga, an Ojibwe woman descended from a well-known fur trade family of mixed European, African, and Ojibwe ancestry. Field matrons assigned to the Great Lakes had direct contact with the community, more so than the agency physicians, and Bonga and her colleagues held complex and nuanced opinions of Ojibwe families. Day-to-day experiences within Ojibwe homes taught them to appreciate the valuable contributions women made to community health.

As other scholars have noted, field matrons also documented the social life of Indian communities in the early twentieth century. Josephine Bonga's written surveys provided rich details about tribal economies, household conditions, family life, and health. She witnessed Ojibwe survival through years of intense hardship. Bonga and other field matrons came face to face with sickness, disability, and poverty, but they also noted the considerable efforts of Ojibwe labor. In particularly vivid detail, they described women's work at fishing, picking blueberries and cranberries, gardening, making maple sugar, and gathering wild rice. Field matrons were among the first health care workers to warn of the threat posed by returned boarding school students, who appeared to be the main carriers of tuberculosis and trachoma within Ojibwe communities. Bonga and her colleagues would have been aware of the persistence of tribal spiritual traditions—that Ojibwe people had not given up their "grand medicine ideas."[22]

Documenting the Partnership of Plants and Music

There were other intelligent observers of Ojibwe life in the early reservation era. Frances Densmore carried out fieldwork among Ojibwe people in the early twentieth century. As a scholar and ethnomusicologist, Densmore began researching Ojibwe music in 1905, when she made her first trip to the Grand Portage Reservation on Lake Superior in northern Minnesota. As a young woman, Densmore attended Oberlin Conservatory of Music, was deeply impressed with the work of pioneer ethnographer Alice Fletcher on Omaha music, and knew something about Dakota culture from her years growing up in Red Wing, Minnesota. Her collaborations in the field with Ojibwe people at Leech Lake, Red Lake, and White Earth in 1906–09 allowed Densmore to transcend her limited education, mature as a scholar, and carve out a place for herself within the new discipline of anthropology. By 1910, when she published her first major study, *Chippewa Music*, Densmore was already a professional "collaborator" with the Bureau of American Ethnology. She held that position, working with and studying Ojibwe people, until her death in 1957 at the age of ninety.[23]

Early on, Densmore appreciated that Ojibwe people organize their world with plants and music coexisting in symbiotic partnership. Already a passionate student of Indian music, Densmore found that her fieldwork made her increasingly attentive to Ojibwe plant knowledge. She eventually made trips to most of Minnesota's Ojibwe reservations, as well as Lac Courte Oreilles in Wisconsin and Manitou Rapids in Ontario. Her fieldwork resulted in a breakthrough discussion of American Indian ethnobotany that she titled "Uses of Plants by the Chippewa Indians." Exposure to the Ojibwe world view taught Densmore to appreciate the relationship between Ojibwe use of local plants and the Ojibwe people's musical tradition. Referring colleagues to her earlier articles on music, Densmore explained, "Herbs were used in the treatment of the sick and in the working of charms, and songs were sung to make the treatment and the charms effective."[24]

After her landmark trip in 1905, Densmore engaged in two astonishingly productive decades of fieldwork, during which she interacted with women in particular. Essential to interpreting her field experiences, published work, and scholarly legacy today is the recognition that more than half of the sixty-three people she named as informants for her articles about Ojibwe plant knowledge were women. In "Uses of Plants," Densmore wrote, "A majority of the informants on this subject were women," and acknowledged that "both men and women related the uses of plants in medicine, economic life, and the useful and decorative arts."[25]

As informants, interpreters, and friends, Ojibwe women contributed significantly to Densmore's successful career. Mary Warren English, who lived on the White Earth Reservation, played a critical role in a decade and a half of Densmore's fieldwork. English served as Densmore's principal interpreter beginning in 1907 and facilitated Densmore's fieldwork for the next fifteen years. While working as an interpreter, she introduced Densmore to many of the remarkable practitioners of holistic medicine in Ojibwe communities. English had many contacts at Red Lake, where she taught school for fifteen years and married her husband, John English. English's home, White Earth, was rich in medicinal herbs, making it an ideal location for Densmore to acquire plant specimens.

Densmore was fortunate to gain the friendship of Mary Warren English—and that of her remarkable extended kin. The Warrens of White Earth were a family of French, English, and Ojibwe ancestry with a long history at Madeline Island, which was named for their grandmother. Descendants of White Crane, the hereditary chief at LaPointe, they had arrived at White Earth during the removals of 1868–70. Mary Warren English was one of six children and a sister of the extraordinary nineteenth-century historian William W. Warren, author of *History of the Ojibway People*.[26]

Densmore recalled first meeting Julia Spears Warren after re-

Mary Warren English, who worked with Frances Densmore, about 1920.

turning to White Earth for the annual tribal celebration held on June 14, 1907:

> After a few days at the rectory we were invited to the home of Mrs. Charles W. Mee, a niece of William W. Warren, the historian of the tribe. There we remained more than two weeks while I wrote down Chippewa stories and became acquainted with the Indians. Too much appreciation can not be expressed for the aid and encouragement given by Mrs. Mee and her mother, Mrs. Julia Warren Spears, at that time and throughout my work.

Mrs. Mee helped me contact the Indians, often acting as interpreter, her mother related many incidents of historic interest, and her aunt, Mrs. Mary Warren English, was my principal interpreter for more than ten years in my work for the Bureau of American Ethnology.[27]

In Ojibwe Country, Densmore encountered a dynamic network of women who specialized in plants and their healing properties. At White Earth, Red Lake, and elsewhere in northern Minnesota, she grew to appreciate the particular knowledge of women while she organized and classified the dozens and dozens of plants and herbs they gathered. It makes sense that many of the plants Ojibwe women gathered were exclusive to female health issues and wellness. In fact, seventeen of the nearly two hundred plants Densmore identified by their botanical and Ojibwe names were described as medicines for "female diseases," according to her informants. A number of other plants treated menstrual discomforts. One, black cohosh, is prescribed by physicians today and widely used by women in North America and Europe for relief of menopause complaints. Densmore found that Ojibwe women used this same plant for female health. Medicine people harvested many plants in August, manoominikie giizis, the ricing month in the northern Great Lakes. The Ojibwe approach to wellness, linking the body to spiritual and emotional health, was appreciated by very few westerners who encountered American Indians living on reservations in the early twentieth century.[28]

Ojibwe people regard plants as sacred because of their ability to nourish and heal the body. In Ojibwemowin, the term for medicine is mashki akeeng, strength of the earth. Medicine people approached plant and medicinal knowledge in a meticulously systematic way, always emphasizing, as Frances Densmore put it, "experiment and study." Like artists in their work, they were masterful observers of the natural world. They knew the exact time to harvest a multiplicity of plants, a quantity of which had the most ephemeral season. They understood the correct part of the plant to use—roots, stems, or leaves—and also recognized the importance of compounding plants for medicines in some cases. Densmore learned that Ojibwe people liked to augment their diets with a variety of wild plants, many of which were vitamin rich and consumed as teas. Ojibwe people especially liked teas made from the twigs of wild cherry, chokecherry, and red raspberry, or the leaves of wintergreen spruce or snowberry, which they sweetened with maple sugar. Densmore was served a simple Ojibwe beverage of maple sugar dissolved in cold water, which she found "pleasantly refreshing" during a warm summer day in the field. She noted that Ojibwe people were also very fond of "swamp tea," which is still appreciated today for calming stomach ailments and preferred to many of the perhaps more convenient remedies found in drugstores, Wal-Mart, or Indian health clinics. Swamp tea, which Ojibwe people also refer to as muckigobug and commonly called Labrador tea, has the added benefit of providing vitamin C.[29]

After Densmore met the healer Nawajibigokwe, she commented, "Few persons on the White Earth Reservation are more skilled than she in the lore of native medicines." Indeed, Nawajibigokwe was highly regarded in her community for gathering minisinowuck, or island herb medicine, traditionally given to departing warriors. Nawajibigokwe, whose name Densmore translated as "Woman Dwelling in the Midst of the Rocks," composed songs related to this herb. Densmore noted that while Ojibwe people had a number of commonly accepted designations for plants and trees in their environment, "individuals often had their own names for the plants which they used as remedies." Healers sometimes did not reveal a particular plant's name to Densmore.[30]

Densmore visited the most remote of all the Minnesota Indian communities in 1918. Ponemah rises from the water at the point where the upper and lower portions of Red Lake join, forming a vast freshwater lake in northern Minnesota. The community was accessible only by water in summer or by crossing over the frozen ice in winter. There Densmore witnessed firsthand the Ojibwe way of life. Inspired by the dynamic traditions of Ojibwe music she discovered there, she recorded many songs that deeply influenced her ideas about American Indian music and its relationship to healing and medicine. She later wrote about the isolated community, "Most of the Indians are members of the Midewiwin and its rites are closely observed." After visiting Ponemah, Densmore consistently underscored in her writings and lectures that Ojibwe people believe in "the healing power of music." Densmore came to regard her Ojibwe informants, in her words, as "primitive psychologists," because of their ability to harness the spiritual energy of song for emotional health.

Mino bimaadizi, the Good Life

As an ethnographer, Frances Densmore learned to appreciate Ojibwe culture and values through careful study of their plants, medicine, and music. She understood that "health and long life represented the highest good to the mind of the Chippewa, and he who had knowledge conducive to that end was the most highly esteemed among them." In the Great Lakes, manoomin, or wild rice, is the supreme plant, respected in ceremony and daily life. Densmore's "Uses of Plants" presented an unusually rich ethnography of the traditional wild rice harvest in the Great Lakes, which she explored in other publications, including *Chippewa Customs*.[31]

When Densmore visited Ojibwe Country, the traditional wild rice harvest was the domain of women; not until a few decades later did men take over primary responsibility for ricing. Her study thus captures a profoundly different historic era in Ojibwe history when women still controlled the traditional harvest. Densmore attentively described the details of harvesting, from pre-harvest binding of the stalks to the multiple steps of post-harvest pro-

Maple sugaring at Red Lake, 1939.

cessing. She concluded simply, "The rice was harvested by the women," and her valuable photographs capture Ojibwe women at every stage of production.[32]

Densmore observed a similarly important role for Ojibwe women in maple syrup cultivation. Women set up seasonal camps, where they put as many as two thousand taps into large stands of maple trees to render great quantities of watery sap to its amber liquid form every spring. Densmore, fascinated by this annual event, described the Ojibwe sugar bush in vivid ethnographic detail. Even before other family members came to the sugar bush, the women had carefully prepared for the cheerful labor of making maple syrup. Densmore wrote,

> Arriving at the camp, the women shoveled the snow away from the sugar lodge and soon made themselves comfortable. A ladder of tree branches was among the articles stored during the winter, and placing this against the framework of the lodge they ascended and spread their rolls of birch bark on the roof. On the platforms in the interior of the lodge they spread cedar boughs, if such were

available, and on these were laid rush mats, over which
were spread blankets and warm furs. The storehouse was
opened, the great rolls of birch bark being turned back,
one at a time, until beneath the weather-worn coverings
were seen the heaps of bark dishes, makuks, and buckets,
white outside and warm yellow within, others a soft gray
or dulled by age to a rich mahogany color. The odor of
balsam and dry sweet birch bark came from the lodge.
There was also a supply of birch bark for making new
utensils, if such were necessary. The material which the
women brought with them from the winter camps depended, of course, on their knowledge of what had been
left in the storing lodge the previous season.[33]

Ojibwe women were precise about the role of weather in the
science of maple sugar cultivation. As they went about their seasonal labor, the women with whom Densmore worked told her,
"the best sugar was made when the early part of the winter had
been open, allowing the ground to freeze deeper than usual, this
being followed by deep snow. They considered the first run of
sap as best. Their other observations were that a storm usually
followed the first warm weather, and afterwards the sap began
to flow again. This sap, however, grained less easily than the first
and had a slightly different flavor. Rain produced a change in the
taste and a thunderstorm is said to have destroyed the characteristic flavor of the sugar."[34]

Ojibwe women had many uses for maple syrup. It seasoned
fruits, vegetables, cereals, and fish and was sometimes reduced
to thick syrup for compounding with medicines to suit the deli-
cate palates of children. The sugar itself was candy. Densmore
wrote, "a woman with a goodly supply of maple sugar in its various forms was regarded as a thrifty woman providing for the
wants of her family."[35]

Densmore's ethnography revealed a remarkable tradition of

plant and medicinal knowledge hidden within the tiny Indian communities of the Great Lakes. Wild rice and maple sugar were the essential foods. Sweet grass was important for ceremony. Lady's-slipper was a toothache remedy, butternut a popular dye. Plant names sometimes had interesting Ojibwe cultural references, such as one taken for rheumatism called "Nanabozhoo's grandmother's hair." Ojibwe people used plants and medicines every day for minor bodily complaints like headache or sore throat and occasionally for serious medical conditions. Densmore met Maiingans, an Ojibwe man who related the story of his childhood leg amputations after a severe case of frostbite. His surgeon was an Ojibwe healer who dressed the wounds twice a day with pounded bark. Densmore wrote with admiration, "the healing was perfect." Densmore later observed that working with plants and healing was gender-neutral labor in Ojibwe culture: "All summer the old medicine men and women were gathering and drying herbs so they would have a good supply of medicines and remedies of all sorts."[36]

While Densmore's ethnography was highly attentive to the stability of Ojibwe traditions in the early twentieth century, it was less attuned to the ways in which politics and American colonization were challenging Ojibwe survival in the Great Lakes. Most of her fieldwork came just prior to the emergence of the Jingle Dress Dance, and Densmore never mentioned the practice in her published work or public conversation. But political change brought Densmore's work more attention during the 1930s, a decade of unprecedented popular interest in American Indian culture in the United States. Anthropologists and intellectuals, as well as politicians in Washington, were distancing themselves from ideas of progress based on race and turning away from long-standing policies of cultural assimilation exemplified by the allotment of reservations and boarding school education. In that decade, John Neihardt interviewed Black Elk in South Dakota and Oliver La Farge won a Pulitzer Prize for his

Indian novel *Laughing Boy*. Museums collected American Indian artifacts by the thousands. Densmore herself presented a series about American Indian life in Minnesota on WCCO Radio in Minneapolis during the winter and spring of 1932, introducing Minnesotans to aspects of Dakota and Ojibwe culture they might not otherwise experience.[37]

In the century since Densmore embarked on her important fieldwork among Ojibwe people, interest in Native landscapes and the environment and traditions of Indigenous healing has never been greater. Indigenous people throughout North America and the world are remembering their traditional diets, activities, and medicines along with linguistic and cultural revitalizations. The "healing power of music" is no longer a belief confined to American Indians.[38]

Healing and Renewal: Ojibwe Women, Nursing, and the Influenza of 1918

While Ojibwe women were practicing their healing ways on early twentieth-century reservations, historical documents show Ojibwe women also spreading into towns and urban areas, some gaining a foothold by working in one of the few occupations available to women of all backgrounds: nursing. A number of early twentieth-century Indian boarding schools had nursing programs, and Indian nurses were often very dedicated to their profession, while others fell into nursing for a shorter period as the demand for female workers exploded once the global epidemic of influenza reached the United States. Numbers of these workers were described as "volunteers," mothers and wives temporarily working outside of the home as the need became critical, but others were young and single, and the flu epidemic presented an opportunity for them, a pathway into an adventurous new life. The latter was the case for Lutiant LaVoye, a volunteer as fresh faced as she was strong willed, a June graduate of the Haskell Indian Boarding School in Lawrence, Kansas, who arrived in Washington, DC, in the fall of 1918.

I noticed this "volunteer nurse" a few years ago while looking at an online collection of historical documents and photographs about the big flu curated by the National Archives. I was impressed with a letter LaVoye had written while working at a military hospital in Washington, DC, to a friend back at the Haskell Indian Boarding School. The letter is dated October 17, 1918; most of the deaths from the pandemic took place during a sixteen-week period from September to December of 1918. The letter is posted on the National Archives website not so much because of its value to Indian history but for how richly it describes the events and social history of the epidemic's peak in the United States. The volunteer nurse experienced the worst of the epidemic firsthand. After reading her remarkable letter, I wondered, "Who was she? What was her tribe? And, *did she survive the epidemic?*" I was especially concerned because so many victims of the 1918–19 flu were atypically young, and influenza is considered more virulent and worrisome to public health when it is deadly to young people.[39]

As with so many fascinating documents we come across doing research, there was only one piece of solid information: her signature, "Lutiant." Luckily for me, this wonderful letter writer had an unusual name. After finding Lutiant LaVoye in the pages of the Haskell newspaper, I went looking for her in U.S. census records. I found Lutiant at age ten, living in Roseau, Minnesota, a town that borders the Red Lake Reservation, on the U.S. and Canadian border. Lutiant was Ojibwe!

Ojibwe people in the Great Lakes and northern Mississippi River area, like Lutiant's own family, experienced a historic low in their population around 1900, and the early twentieth century was a time of dispossession and widespread social disruption on reservations, one with a tragic effect on family life. I learned a few basic facts of LaVoye's life from the 1910 census and from the

A portrait of Lutiant LaVoye printed in The Indian Leader, *published by the Haskell Indian School.*

death records of family members. She lived with her stepfather, Fred LaVoye, age forty-three, who had been born in "French Canada" and was described in the census as "white" and "English speaking." The census also showed a young wife in the household, Delia, who was just twenty-three and also "English speaking." Lutiant was the oldest of four children, and Delia and all the children are listed as "Indian."

Death records indicated Lutiant's mother, whose surname was Grandbois, had died in 1905, when Lutiant would have been five or six years old, and her death was followed by an infant's death five months later. It appeared the baby outlived Lutiant's mother for a short time. This tragedy was probably the reason for Lutiant's wardship with an uncle at White Earth, her subsequent schooling at St. Benedict's, a Catholic girl's school in Minnesota that accepted Indians, and her eventual placement in two government boarding schools, Genoa in Nebraska, and later Haskell.

When Lutiant LaVoye entered boarding school, there was discussion among the school and reservation superintendents about her tribal citizenship, questions concerning her parentage and whether or not she met any blood quantum for enrollment in an Indian school. They conferred with White Earth and Turtle Mountain and decided she was not enrolled at any agency. This conclusion was not surprising, considering the status of Ojibwe people who lived outside the boundaries of the Red Lake Reservation. In a document from Haskell, this is how Lutiant herself described her childhood and education:

> My full name is Lutiant Ruth Verne La Voye. I was born on our country home, in northern Minnesota, near Canada, in 1899. I lived with my parents until Mother died in 1905, then with my maternal grandparents until my adoption by David Van Wert in 1911 [one year after the census described the household in Roseau]. All my school days were spent in public white schools in Minnesota and Canada and three years at St. Benedict's Academy in Southern Minnesota, until four years ago (1914) when I attended my first Indian school, at Genoa, Nebraska. I attended school there only one year, finishing the eighth grade, then went to Haskell Institute. I took up the Business course and I am now in the graduating class. (I have had a little of the first and second year High School work, and studied French, Latin, and Music a short time while at the Academy.) I speak French and English, but have never learned to speak the Indian language of my tribe or any other tribe. *I have always had a great desire of becoming an efficient stenographer, to live on my own resources, and to be independent* [emphasis added].

On October 17, 1918, when Lutiant was nineteen and working as a volunteer nurse in Washington, she wrote to her friend Louise, back at Haskell.

213-14th St. South East,
October 17, 1918

Dear friend Louise:

So everybody has the "Flu" at Haskell? I wish to
goodness Miss Keck and Mrs. McK. would get it and die with
it. Really, it would be such a good riddance, and not much lost
either! As many as 90 people die every day here with the
"Flu". Soldiers too, are dying by the dozens. So far, Felicity, C.
Zane, and I are the only ones of the Indian girls who have not
had it. We certainly consider ourselves lucky too, believe me.
Kathrine and I just returned last Sunday evening from Camp
Humphreys "Somewher[e] in Virginia" where we volunteered
to help nurse soldiers sick with the Influenza. We were there
at the Camp ten days among some of the very worse cases
and yet we did not contract it. We had intended staying much
longer than we did, but the work was entirely too hard for us,
and anyway the soldiers were all getting better, so we came
home to rest up a bit. We were day nurses and stationed in the
Officer's barracks for six days and then transferred to the
Private's barracks or hospital and were there four days before
we came back. All nurses were required to work twelve hours
a day--we worked from seven in the morning until seven at
night, with only a short time for luncheon and dinner.

Believe me, we were always glad when night came
because we sure did get tired. We had the actual Practical
nursing to do--just like the other nurses had, and were given
a certain number of wards with three or four patients in each
of them to look after. Our chief duties were to give medicines
to the patients, take temperatures, fix ice packs, feed them at
"eating time", rub their back or chest with camphorated sweet
oil, make egg-nogs, and a whole string of other things I can't
begin to name. I liked the work just fine, but it was too hard,
not being used to it. When I was in the Officer's barracks, four
of the officers of whom I had charge, died. Two of them were
married and called for their wife nearly all the time. It was
sure pitiful to see them die. I was right in the wards alone with
them each time, and Oh! The first one that died sure unnerved
me--I had to go to the nurses' quarters and cry it out. The

other three were not so bad. Really, Louise, Orderlies carried
the dead soldiers out on stretchers at the rate of two every
three hours for the first two days [we] were there. Two German
spies, posing as doctors, were caught giving these Influenza
germs to the soldiers and they were shot last Saturday morning
at sunrise. It is such a horrible thing, it is hard to believe and
yet such things happen almost every day in Washington.

Repeated calls come from the Red Cross for nurses to do
district work right here in D.C. I volunteered again, but as yet I
have not been called and am waiting. Really, they are certainly
"hard up" for nurses--even me can volunteer as a nurse in a
camp or in Washington. There are about 300 soldiers stationed
at Potomac Park right her[e] in D.C. just a short distance from
the Interior building where I work, and this morning's paper
said that the deaths at this Park were increasing, so if fortune
favors me, I may find myself there before the week is ended.

I have a very dear soldier friend who is stationed there--
Lieut. Cantril by name. 'Twas so funny how we first met. I was
completely lost in St. Louis at the Union station (On my way to
D.C.) and simply had no idea where I was going--just wandering
around the station to pass away my 3½ hrs. there waiting for
my train. Finally, I thought of sending Odile a telegram so she
could be at the station to meet me. I went to the Postal office
right there in the Station and this soldier was standing there
waiting to send a telegram too. I waited, waited, and waited
and could not get in to send one, so I picked up my suit case and
traveling bag and started towards the Ladies' Waiting room.
Instead of taking my own traveling bag, I left mine and picked
up this soldier's bag. They were as much alike as two peas, and
I was so tired I never took special notice, but I thought I had
my own bag. When I opened it to get out my comb and powder--
behold! There was a kit-bag fully equip[p]ed and a knitted
sweater in it, plus a few other trinkets'. I knew then, whose bag
I had, so checked my suit case and started out to look for this
soldier and exchange bags, as I thought he had mine. After
walking around 45 minutes I began to despair of ever finding
him and started back to the Ladies room and I came upon him
sitting in one corner. I recognized my bag right away and went

to exchange. He was simply so tickled to get his bag back he almost squeezed the life out of my hand when he shook it. I had my card and destination tacked on the handle of my bag, so he found out where I was going without telling him--and as fate would have it--he was going to D.C. too, so we traveled the rest of the way together. He is a perfect gentlemen, and sure treated me nice on the way. Since I am located here, he has been down to our house twice to see me since I came back from Camp Humphreys, and he sure wants me to come down to Potomac Park as a nurse. He is not what one would call "handsome" but he is certainly good-looking, and on top of all that--he is a CATHOLIC. Sure like it for myself too. All the girls have soldiers here--Indian girls also. Some of the girls have soldiers and sailors too. The boys are particularly crazy about the Indian girls. They tell us that the Indian girls are not so "easy" as the white girls, so I guess maybe that's their reason.

Washington is certainly a beautiful place. There is so much to be said in favor of it, that if I started, I don't believe I should ever get through. Odile and I have to pass by the Capitol, the Union Station, the War Department, the Pension Bldg., and through the noted Lincoln park every morning on our way to work. The Washington Monument (555 ft. high) is within walking distance of the Interior Department (where we work) and we walked there last evening after work. It certainly is high and we are planning to go up in the elevator some time to look over the city. We were going last evening, but the place is closed temporarily, on account of this "Flu".

The Aviation field is another very interesting place here. Air-plaines fly over the city at all hours of the day now, and sometimes so low that one can hear the noise of the machine.

Besides Aviators, we have hundreds of soldiers, sailors, Marines, French "Blue Devils" and even the National band of Italy her[e] in Washington. Douglas Fairbanks and Geraldine Farrar are here also on the fourth Liberty Loan campaign and I was privileged to take a chance to peep at them. Just yesterday, Douglas sold ONE MILLION DOLLARS WORTH OF BONDS FOR WASHINGTON. It was rumoured that Washington was going to fail to reach its quota in Liberty Bonds on account of having so many deaths and sick people in the city, but the way "Doug" is selling 'em, it doesn't seem as if it will. A lot of the girls from the Office here go out to sell bonds but some of them dont make much of a success. One of the Indian girls, named Cathryne Welch, went out last week to sell bonds and she sold so many that she got escused from the Office for the rest of this week to do nothing but sell bonds. She is a very pretty girl--a high school graduate and one year normal. She has two brothers in the army--one is a Captain and the other a Sargeant. Maybe you remember seeing Capt. Gus Welch's picture in the K.C. Star--well that is her brother and he is "over there" now.

All the schools, churches, theaters, dancing halls, etc., are closed here also. There is a bill in the Senate today authorizing all the war-workers to be released from work for the duration of this epidemic. It has not passed the house yet, but I can't help but hope it does. If it does, Lutiant can find plenty of things at home to busy herself with, or she might accidentally take a trip to Potomac Park. Ha! Ha!

It is perfectly alright about the sweater. I don't expect you to be able to get it while you are quar[an]tined, but will still be glad to have it if you can send it as soon as you are out of quartined. It is rather cold in Washington, but not cold enough to wear winter coats yet, and my suit coat is a little too thin, so I figured out that a sweater would be the thing to have. Sometimes it is cold enough to wear a wrap while working, but of course it is out of the question to work in a heavy winter coat. However, send it whenever you find it convenient to do so, and I will settle with you as promptly as possible.

Well Louise, if you are not dead tired reading this letter, I'll write another like it some other time. There is still a lot I could tell you about D.C., but it's nearing lunch time and I want to be right there on the dot, as I always am--to be sure.

Write again whenever you find it convenient to do so-- always glad to hear the Haskell news from you.

Sincerely your friend,
Lutiant.

Address same as before.

Lutiant's opening lines are incredibly mischievous: "So everybody has the 'Flu' at Haskell? I wish to goodness Miss Keck and Mrs. McK. [her former teachers] would get it and die with it. Really, it would be such good riddance, and not much lost either!" She then describes her work at the military hospital during the epidemic, introducing the most significant and serious aspects of her narrative and making it an important historical document of the global epidemic. She is a terrific writer, blending humor easily with incredibly serious and vivid descriptions of the epidemic's toll on the people who are living, and dying, in Washington. As a young woman of nineteen writing to a girlfriend, having her first taste of freedom, she must also detour into her romantic interests, especially a soldier she met while traveling. (In the movies they call this "meeting cute.") Lutiant's observations on dating reflect her encounter with a perspective on Indian womanhood that differs from views usual at the time: "They tell us that the Indian girls are not so 'easy' as the white girls." But most importantly of all, she describes wartime Washington and the terrible impact of the epidemic. And after seven wonderful pages to Louise, so descriptive, like a little movie, the letter ends with mention of the quarantine taking place at Haskell, and how she always likes to hear the Haskell news.

Lutiant would later regret her opening lines. Boarding school mail was often screened, and the letter was passed around at Haskell. The superintendent wrote to Lutiant, and her supervisor in Washington was informed of the letter. Lutiant later wrote a deeply apologetic letter back to Haskell. Boarding schools allowed for little privacy in correspondence.

Lutiant had spent weeks in the thick of a global pandemic. She had worked intimately among patients, otherwise young and healthy, whom she saw die. I worried she had also died. In fact, I was anxious when I received her thick Haskell student file from the National Archives. After all the hardship Lutiant had experienced: mother dead, a wardship that she chafed under, mixed feelings about boarding school (evident in other letters in her school file), did she get to live the life of a stenographer that she wrote about at Haskell?

Then, this last letter from Lutiant, to Haskell, dated September 20, 1923: "I wish to enter George Washington University in October, and find that I am short a few credits which I thought possibly could be made up from the subjects I took up at Haskell. I shall appreciate if you will have the enclosed form, or a similar one, filled out and returned to me at an early date in order that there may be no delay in presenting it at the University in time to enter the classes October 1st."

City directories from Washington in the early 1920s show several apartment addresses for a Lutiant LaVoye, occupation *Stenographer.* The trail runs cold here, after 1923, but I like to think she lived a long and wonderful life (on her own resources and very independently) and that possibly she married and changed her name.

Jingle Dress Dancers in the Modern World

As scholars including Philip Deloria have noted, we sometimes make "the dangerous assumption that reservation and rural people were not themselves also part of modernity." If we imagine a jingle dress dancer in 1918, living on a reservation in rural Minnesota or Ontario, as only following an older tradition and not part of making the modern world, we would have to ignore how creatively Ojibwe women responded to the global epidemic. Decades after the tradition first developed, my grandmother Jeanette and other Ojibwe women regarded the dress, dance, and songs associated with the Jingle Dress Dance as treasures of our cultural heritage.

As I have thought more about the horrific circumstances that led to the emergence of the Jingle Dress Dance, new yet deeprooted traditions of healing among Ojibwe women, and the story of a young Ojibwe nurse in the flu epidemic, I find meaningful parallels. By 1918 in the Ojibwe Great Lakes, the immediate effects of settler-colonialism had peaked. Dispossession was rampant, the population was declining under an epidemic, and cultural and spiritual practices were under surveillance, just as assimilation was promoted as the alternative to an Ojibwe way of life. My own family and the scattered relatives of the young nurse, Lutiant LaVoye, experienced many of these problems firsthand. She was living in Ojibwe Country (Roseau, Minnesota) but on land that no longer belonged to the Red Lake Ojibwe. Her mother was dead. With too many mouths to feed, her French Canadian stepfather sent her to relatives, and they sent her to boarding school. Right before Haskell, she was living on the White Earth Reservation—where other families had the same problems.

Perhaps it is easier to see a young nurse, especially one registered as just barely meeting the minimum standard of blood quantum for attending a federal Indian school, one who grew up in northern Minnesota but in a town rather than on a reservation, stepping onto a train platform in the fall of 1918 in the Midwest as a progressive, possibly somewhat assimilated, example of modern Indian womanhood. Maybe more modern than a jingle dress dancer—but we would be wrong about that. Lutiant survived the epidemic. The first jingle dress dancer is also a survivor. To me, Lutiant LaVoye's story is a fascinating fragment within a broader narrative about the survival and resiliency of Ojibwe women's lives and accomplishments during a critical moment in Ojibwe history, and world history. Just when Ojibwe women, and their communities, seem to have reached bottom, they also reached into the most creative and compassionate places in their souls to pick themselves up. That they did so during a global epidemic is perhaps the least remarkable part of their story.

5

My Grandfather's Knocking Sticks
Labor, Gender, and the Great Depression

My grandfather's knocking sticks were hand carved out of cedar, elegantly smooth, and lightweight. I was a girl when my mother first showed me the weathered pair of sticks, the kind Great Lakes Ojibwe people prefer when harvesting wild rice. They belonged to her father, Fred Auginash. The cedar sticks were the only personal possessions of my grandfather that I recall ever having seen, except for his military discharge papers from World War I. When Ojibwe people die, loved ones distribute their belongings within the extended family and community, and it was remarkable to have personal items after so many years. My mother demonstrated the firm, rhythmic *swish swish* motion of knocking rice from stalks into the canoe as she showed them to me. She hung the sticks on the wall for a time, fitting treatment for a treasured family heirloom, but I forgot about them, unconcerned with the cultural livelihood and history the knocking sticks represented.

Ojibwe people call wild rice manoomin, the good seed that grows in water. Manoomin varies slightly in size and color, but it is always perfect. It is a sacred food intertwined in countless ways with Ojibwe spiritual practices, kinship relations, economies, gender roles, history, place, and contemporary existence. Naming feasts for infants and children always include wild rice, as do wakes and funerals and every meaningful cultural event in between birth and death. Indigenous people have harvested the freshwater plant for a thousand years or more, and even now it grows naturally in gentle, mineral-rich waters of the less polluted lakes and river headwaters of Minnesota, Wisconsin, Manitoba, and Ontario. Scientists call it *Zizania aquatica L.*[1]

Fred Auginash spent his first twenty-five years near Big Sandy Lake in central Minnesota, an Indigenous landscape rich with game, fish, and wild rice where in his youth Ojibwe families faced violence and dispossession. Driven from his home, a fortunate resolution to crisis emerged only after his marriage to my grandmother, which allowed him to settle permanently on the southern shores of lower Red Lake. Because Red Lake's hereditary chiefs and leaders had resisted allotment and insisted on protecting the older ways of communal ownership of property, my people maintained many Indigenous, seasonal economic traditions, and the work site changed with the season. The reservation also preserved native plants and animal life, and the last woodland caribou in Minnesota roamed there as late as 1940. In those years, my grandparents joined other Ojibwe people at sociable wild rice camps every August and September for the demanding work of harvest. Unlike generations of Ojibwe men before him, it appears that my grandfather knocked rice into a canoe with his handsome cedar sticks.[2]

It is important to ask why some American Indian labor was done differently after the era of reservations—especially work that carried considerable cultural significance. For the Ojibwe, the Great Depression of the 1930s transformed the gendered practices associated with the wild rice economy in significant and lasting ways. As in earlier decades, when missionary and U.S. government "civilization" programs sought to make farmers of American Indian men, changes in Ojibwe labor practices were primarily the result of intervention by the state and Indian participation in government work programs of the Works Progress Administration (WPA) and the Civilian Conservation Corps–Indian Division (CCC–ID). The women and men who labored in the wild rice economy of the 1930s were workers with seasonal work sites, fully engaged in modern life. The fact that their ancestors had harvested wild rice for centuries and regarded it as a sacred food does not imply that reservation workers were unprepared to embrace change.[3]

Politics and government programs played a crucial role in the transformation of the Indigenous harvest when the WPA and the CCC–ID and the Minnesota State Forest Service began to organize masculine labor in newfangled "Indian wild rice camps" to reinvigorate the traditional economy with a Western-style work ethic. White bureaucrats who controlled the labor force for government programs were unwilling or unable to recognize the Indigenous harvest as women's work, posing a challenge to the long-standing monopoly Ojibwe women maintained over wild rice practices.

Contemporary Ojibwe people have few memories of a time when men were not central to the labor-intensive work of harvesting wild rice. Men today often partner with other men—brothers, cousins, and friends—just as they might go out on the lake with a favorite fishing buddy. Wild rice harvesting is currently a male or gender-neutral activity, but present-day practice evolved from a pre-reservation Indigenous social and economic system of labor and exchange comprised of family-centered rice camps where women managed and carried out most of the work. A critical transition in Ojibwe labor practices emerged during the 1930s according to harvesters such as James Mustache of the Lac Courte Oreilles Reservation. Men began to harvest wild rice during the Great Depression as part of an economic strategy to enhance family preservation and Indigenous survival.[4]

For generations, harvesting and processing wild rice had been the vocational specialty of Ojibwe, Dakota, and Menominee women workers in the Great Lakes. Ojibwe men fished and hunted waterfowl, and children trod wild rice in the bootaagan to release the kernel from its hull, activities that complemented the substantial efforts of women in the Indigenous harvest. In the twentieth century, men expanded their participation in wild rice production, first as husbands partnered with wives on the lakes, later becoming the primary harvesters and producers.[5]

Women's Labor and the Indigenous Wild Rice Harvest

There is rich evidence in Great Lakes history to support the argument that wild rice was a predominantly female enterprise. *The Rice Gatherers*, Seth Eastman's 1867 painting, hangs in a congressional office building on the grounds of the U.S. Capitol in Washington, DC. Eastman was a military man and artist, remembered today for his large portfolio of American Indian paintings and observations of Indigenous life. His paintings were part of the broader movement in nineteenth-century American art intended to document Indians as they disappeared from the landscape, and his military career was central to that colonial project. From 1830 to 1833, while stationed at Fort Snelling, a frontier post at the confluence of the Minnesota and Mississippi rivers, he interacted extensively with Dakota people, and the body of art he produced offers insights into Indigenous ways of life. In 1830 Eastman entered into a short first marriage with Wakaninajinwin (Stands Sacred Woman), the daughter of Mahpiyawicasta (Cloud Man), a Mdewankanton Dakota leader. Eastman's 1867 watercolor, while not a correct ethnographic portrayal of Indigenous methods of harvest, does present three Native women knocking rice from a canoe, with another female figure in the background. Eastman's second wife, Euroamerican writer Mary Henderson Eastman, who had accompanied him to Fort Snelling when he returned as commandant in the 1840s, later wrote text to accompany many of her husband's watercolors and engravings. Her commentary on *The Rice Gatherers* noted that gathering and preparing wild rice were crucial to "the education of an Indian woman," and she provided a spirited and colorful description of the Indigenous harvest.[6]

Firsthand historical accounts and ethnographic literature recorded women's labor in the rice harvest. Between 1820 and the 1850s, Pierre-Esprit Radisson described Dakota women ricing, George Catlin noted that pairs of women worked together in the harvest, and Henry Schoolcraft held that hulling was

Women ricing at White Earth, about 1910, photographed by Frances Densmore.

the only part of production to involve men. "Mary's mother—grandmother and others are about to leave the Lake to get wild rice," wrote Indian agent Lawrence Taliaferro in an 1839 letter regarding his Anglo-Dakota daughter, who lived at Cloud Man's village on Lake Calhoun in present-day Minneapolis. In the late nineteenth century, Joseph Gilfillan, an Episcopal missionary in Minnesota visiting a rice camp in the northern part of White Earth Reservation, estimated six hundred Ojibwe women, but no Native men, had gathered for the harvest in September. Anthropologist Albert Jenks, in his seminal study "The Wild Rice Gatherers of the Upper Lakes," based on fieldwork done in 1899, observed Menominee and Ojibwe women as the primary harvesters and finishers of wild rice. He wrote, "All the work of harvesting is done by the women, who, at times, are assisted by the children. The women of more than one family frequently unite their labors and divide the product according to some prearranged agreement or social custom."[7]

Twentieth-century observers of the Indigenous harvest reached the same conclusion about women's labor; at times, they offered detailed descriptions of ricing techniques and practices.

"The rice was harvested by the women," Frances Densmore stated simply in her classic works of ethnology, and her collection of photographs taken among Ojibwe communities in Minnesota and Wisconsin portray Ojibwe women and their labor at every stage of production. An agronomist for the U.S. Department of Agriculture, Charles E. Chambliss, noted that another name for wild rice is "squaw rice" after he visited Minnesota lakes and published a government circular in 1922. In his masterful study of modern Ojibwe labor and cultural practices associated with wild rice, Thomas Vennum, Jr., suggests, "until fairly recently only women harvested wild rice."[8]

Ojibwe oral tradition and written sources confirm the observations of westerners. The natural resources of Leech Lake "abounds in wild rice in large quantities, of which the Indian women gather sufficient for the winter consumption of their families," wrote nineteenth-century Ojibwe historian William W. Warren. Maude Kegg, born in 1904, grew up with a multilayered understanding of Ojibwe stories and values as well as of methods associated with the Indigenous harvest, all provided by her grandmother, Margaret Pine. Kegg remembered that after her grandmother had completed the laborious steps of processing the wild rice, before anyone was allowed to eat the new rice, she first "gave a feast in which she offered tobacco and talked about the manitous and thunderbirds, and the sun, and all such things, and put tobacco out." And a very long time ago, Nanabozhoo, the famously wayward Ojibwe cultural figure, discovered a lake ripe with grain ready to fall from its stalks. To harvest manoomin, he retrieved his grandma, Nokomis.[9]

The granddaughters of Nokomis were hardworking, creative harvesters. Densmore's fieldwork from 1910 illustrates the skillful patterns of wild rice and maple sugar harvesting practiced by Ojibwe women workers in northern Minnesota and Wisconsin. Typical for Densmore, she made few references to the political turmoil Ojibwe people faced, instead directing her efforts toward documenting aspects of Indigenous culture as she observed them. Her ethnographic photographs of wild rice work sites show women paddling canoes through the rice lakes, poling at the head of a boat, binding stalks of rice pre-harvest, emptying large winnowing trays full of green rice, stirring wild rice on birch-bark mats with long wooden sticks, and sitting before smoky fires to parch the rice. Some work site activities included male family members. Men traveled with their wives and female relatives to help set up seasonal rice and maple sugar camps before departing to fish or hunt ducks, and Densmore photographed men poling rice boats. Children sometimes trod rice. In one of Densmore's illustrations, a boy dances the rice in a cedar-lined bucket, which was put into the hole in the ground that Ojibwe people refer to as the bootaagan, in the final stage of processing, which removed the last chaff from the wild rice. Treading rice in the botaagaan was work commonly performed by many different family members. Historical photographs depict children, men, and even blind Ojibwe individuals dancing the rice. John Rogers, an Ojibwe man born in 1890, mentioned that even though he and his siblings danced in the rice, "The third thrashing, Mother did. She refused to leave this to any of the children."[10]

Binding stalks of rice together, which women did with strips of basswood fiber and later with cloth, was an economic activity of great consequence for Ojibwe women workers, for whom it represented a form of property rights. Densmore was especially attentive to the practice, capturing it on film numerous times and observing, "a field was outlined by stakes, and a woman established her claim to it by going to the field about 10 days before the rice was ripe and tying portions of it in small sheaves." This description suggests women marked their territory on the lakes through binding rice. Menominee women in Wisconsin also expressed prior claims to rice and other property rights through the practice of binding; they "not only controlled the fruits of their labor, the rice, but also probably held the right to a family's ricing bed," according to historian Brian Hosmer.[11]

Mary Razer tying rice with basswood fiber at White Earth, June 1917, photographed by Frances Densmore.

Binding rice stalks had more than one purpose. It allowed canoes to pass more easily, protected the harvest from winds, birds, and foul weather, and allowed the rice to ripen uniformly. It reserved portions of the annual crop for a diverse group of harvesters, especially those community members who riced more slowly because they were elderly or without ricing partners. The last decade in which rice was bound was the transitional 1930s, when men began to join women at the work site, and the practice had completely disappeared by 1940.[12]

Binding rice functioned as one part of an Indigenous legal system to protect wild rice in its unique ecosystem. Also crucial to that legal system was the oshkaabewisag, an elected ricing committee composed of men and women who continued to organize the Indigenous harvest even as the Ojibwe struggled for rights and fought for survival on diminished lands and resources in the Great Lakes. One individual, assigned to signal the opening and length of the harvesting season, also had the authority to levy fees on harvesters who infringed on the orderly rules. Jim Clark, a Mille Lacs Ojibwe born in 1918, explained how women controlled the social organization of the Indigenous harvest on the upper lakes of the Rum River: "There is a piece of land on the east shore of Rice Lake that I believe my mom's grandmother had for a campsite at ricing time," and she "always had the say about who would camp there." When the Mille Lacs region emerged as a contact zone of lumbermen, settlers, and Indigenous inhabitants, the Ojibwe continually defended their treaty rights, their sovereignty, and the integrity of the wild rice lakes.[13]

Labor Relationships in the Contact Zone

Fur traders, missionaries, and early settlers ate Indigenous-harvested wild rice provisioned by Ojibwe and other tribal women when they arrived in the Great Lakes, and they commented on its fine taste and nourishing qualities. Lumbermen from Maine who came to Minnesota in the middle of the nineteenth century also ate wild rice, and, as they paddled their canoes, they were impressed by the miles of lakeshore where Ojibwe people had set

Wild rice tied for harvest, Lake Onamia, 1909.

up their wild rice camps and by the volume of wild rice women workers had stored away for winter. But these immigrants displayed only a mild interest in Indigenous wild rice production.[14]

Although scholars have repeatedly viewed the economic relationships of Indigenous people as being primarily for subsistence, especially patterns of production where women were involved, Indigenous people exchanged goods and foods with traders, settlers, and other new arrivals. Anthropologist Patricia Albers has remarked, "new scholarship is dispelling the notion that tribes were embedded exclusively in subsistence economies, presenting compelling evidence of the complex ways in which American Indians engaged in labor that both sustained their own communities and provisioned foreigners in their midst." Women workers supplied wild rice and manufactured moccasins for loggers, and they were involved in relationships of labor and exchange with Native and non-Native individuals from outside their communities. Their essential labor supported their own people and was crucial to the comfort and survival of immigrants to the Great Lakes.[15]

Newcomers to the wild rice district presumed that agricultural expansion and the burgeoning timber industry were the best uses of the land, and they established a way of life that was destructive to the wild rice habitat and that positioned Ojibwe people on the margins. This presumption had tremendous impact on all aspects of the seasonal round. Ojibwe laborers at Mille Lacs and other reservations were compelled to abandon the economic resources they relied on for survival when dangerous new forms of state regulation of hunting and fishing emerged, or suffer the consequences, a phenomenon scholar Bruce White has referred to as "criminalizing the seasonal round." In the 1890s, middle-class sportsmen in Minnesota succeeded in their long campaign to establish the game-warden system, the predecessor to the Department of Natural Resources, beginning the enforcement of game and fish laws that fined, jailed, and penalized Indigenous people and poor immigrants who hunted and fished for their economic livelihood rather than sport. The Ojibwe were frequently victims of local law authorities bent on Indian removal during this era, and in one notorious 1902 case the Mille Lacs county sheriff forced Ojibwe families off their lands near Isle, Minnesota, marched the band members to a public highway, and set their houses on fire. Trespass laws were a means to inhibit Ojibwe hunting, fishing, and gathering and had a chilling effect on treaty rights. In the spring of 1894, Mille Lacs Ojibwe harvesters including John Skinaway and his wife moved to their seasonal maple sugar camp. John Skinaway, arrested for trespassing in his own country, went to trial in the local non-Indian town and received a sentence of thirty days in jail. Ojibwe laborers returning from seasonal work sites to find their homes occupied by non-Indian squatters had little legal recourse in local courts invested in newly established state policies that patently ignored prior treaty rights as well as the inherent sovereign and aboriginal rights of the original Indigenous landowners.[16]

Workers who supported their families and sustained a rich community life through a seasonal round of gathering wild rice, hunting, fishing, making maple sugar, and gardening were routinely fined and thrown into jail. Minnesota and Wisconsin game wardens enforced the new state regulations in full violation of treaty-based hunting, fishing, and gathering rights. Historian Joan Jensen found that Ojibwe in Wisconsin faced arrest by game wardens as early as 1897. In that year, two elderly male hunters, one seventy-two and the other eighty-eight and blind, were arrested for possessing venison in violation of state game laws and incarcerated for four months in Iron County. State-sanctioned interventions onto tribal homelands and resources intensified in the post-allotment years, and it was usually men who faced unjust arrest, harassment, fines, and jail terms for trespass and violations of fish and game laws. In the Iron County imprisonments case, one hunter's elderly wife was not jailed, yet she faced the cruel hardship of finding her own way home to Lac du Flambeau with the added stress of her husband's incarceration. Game laws in Minnesota and Wisconsin supported the lifeways and desires of middle-class sportsmen and tourists, not Indigenous families who relied on a seasonal round.[17]

Through their labor, Ojibwe women had constructed a complex and orderly system of ecological guardianship to manage the wild rice economy, now jeopardized by infringements on Indigenous land tenure and damages to human and natural resources in the contact zone. Wild rice grows well in waters with gentle currents and steady water levels. Even heavy rains can cause crop failure, and dam construction is lethal. Lumbermen in Canada and the United States built dams to control flow, using large water releases to float logs downstream to be milled. In the mid-nineteenth century, a lumber dam erected on Minnesota's Rum River raised water levels for smaller lakes where Mille Lacs Ojibwe harvested rice, ruining a significant portion of their annual harvest. The Northern States Power Company's creation of the Chippewa River flowage in Wisconsin during the years 1921–24 proved destructive to the rice stands used by Lake Superior bands of Ojibwe. The flowage, built for flood control along the Chippewa River, inundated homelands of the Lac Courte Oreilles Ojibwe who lived at the headwaters, destroying not only villages and graves but also their wild rice. Similarly, work by the U.S. Army Corps of Engineers devastated native wild rice stands at the Minnesota headwaters of the Mississippi River, and dam construction and other alterations since the 1880s caused wild rice that once thrived along the river to decline. "Government and industry control of water levels has in nearly every instance proven disastrous to wild rice crops," Thomas Vennum has compellingly argued. The Ojibwe had no choice but to take allotments on reservations and develop new patterns of labor that included colonial capitalism.[18]

Tourism and Post-allotment Labor History

Ojibwe people created a way of life in the Great Lakes that carefully balanced an economy of seasonally changing work sites and complementary labor for men and women. Female collectives organized the labor of harvesting wild rice and maple sugar. As important as wild rice was to a cycle of seasonal occupations famously described by one Ojibwe woman in the early twentieth century as "very systematic," the Ojibwe never relied on this resource alone, always keeping in mind the possibility of hardship or misfortune.[19]

By the 1920s, Ojibwe workers in the Great Lakes had clearly added another type of seasonal work to their annual cycle—tourism. Ojibwe labor was at the center of a new economy in a developing recreation landscape. Small businesses attracted Indigenous laborers from reservations, and they earned income near their homes and communities. Workers in northern Wisconsin found summer employment at Cardinal's Resort, the Ojibwa Lodge, and Hill's Resort near the Lac du Flambeau Reservation, a community that developed an early appreciation for the rewards of tourism. Women and teenagers cooked, cleaned, and did laundry, while men worked as hunting and fishing guides. Women workers also supported tourism in northern Wisconsin and Minnesota by supplying wild rice, syrup, and berries for summer vacationers, in addition to manufacturing and selling crafts and handiwork large and small, from miniature beadwork trinkets to elaborate birch-bark and porcupine-quill baskets. Husband and wife entrepreneurs Benedict and Margaret Gauthier were the proprietors of Lac du Flambeau's successful "modern summer hotel and cottages," Gauthier's Resort on Long Lake. Sisters Bessie Stone Fisher and Sarah Stone Gilham rented out their two-story home on Fence Lake to summer visitors from Milwaukee. Twenty-year-old Margaret Snow worked seasonally at the Ojibwa Lodge but in winter found time for making beadwork and moccasins before heading to the sugar bush in the spring.[20]

Married couples on the Lac du Flambeau Reservation in the 1920s who participated in the growing tourist economy still maintained a division of labor within a seasonal cycle not unlike the previous generation. Men manufactured canoes and snowshoes in addition to hunting, trapping, and fishing, while women picked and canned berries, made maple sugar and syrup, and gathered and processed wild rice. Lizzie Young's husband worked as a summer guide, while she "made moccasins, bead work, sugar, syrup, [picked] and [canned] wild berries." This combination of Indigenous seasonal activities along with wages from tourist work allowed families to purchase pianos, sewing machines, or "graphaphones." In a few instances, Ojibwe men gathered wild rice as part of their livelihood, though this probably indicated that they traveled with women to the work site and helped their family set up wild rice camp during the season. Making maple syrup and sugar was also women's work, but some Ojibwe men such as Bob Pine of Lac du Flambeau assisted their wives. During the 1920s, most married couples had children who attended boarding schools or local public schools, an arrangement that may have reduced the number of available hands in the sugar bush. More Lac du Flambeau women went to the early spring sugar bush to make maple syrup than gathered wild rice in late summer, indicating that the labor of maple sugaring may have been more compatible with a local economy increasingly geared toward tourism.[21]

Widowed and divorced women who worked in reservation communities during the 1920s faced a particular set of challenges as high rates of disease and death destabilized kin networks. To accommodate an economic existence without partners, many women workers hunted and fished in addition to raising children and grandchildren. Helen Skye, a boarding school student at Lac du Flambeau, was supported by her sixty-six-year-old grandmother, an active hunter and trapper who also earned income from maple sugar, berries, and wild rice. Similarly, the widowed Margaret Brown gathered wild rice and worked "like a man" by hunting, trapping, and fishing in addition to being the sole caretaker of a mentally disabled son. Mrs. Catfish was a great-grandmother who still went to the sugar bush, picked berries, gathered wild rice, and tanned hides at seventy-eight. Mattice

Scott, a successful midwife with four grown children, practiced the seasonal round in addition to crafting woven bags and reed mats and tanning hides. Perhaps to ease her burden or as a testimony to a zest for life, Scott became a new bride at age sixty-four, John Batiste her Potawatomie groom.[22]

Tourism inspired yet another form of work for Ojibwe people: performance. As anthropologist Larry Nesper has noted, Lac du Flambeau Ojibwe found economic opportunity through staged dance and cultural performance after World War II, a time when tourists again flocked to northern Wisconsin. Tourism was also critical to Ojibwe survival during the Depression years. Guidebooks, advertisements, and postcards from northern resorts and Minnesota's office of tourism suggest that the opportunity to view and interact with Indians was a significant draw for vacationers who traveled to the lakes and woodlands, though genuine contact came most frequently through mundane activity performed by maids or cooks. Entire Ojibwe families performed and worked in summer pageants held at Itasca State Park in Minnesota, a fashionable tourist destination that included the headwaters of the Mississippi River, native stands of red and white pine, sparkling lakes, and the Douglas Lodge. Ojibwe workers from surrounding reservations at White Earth, Leech Lake, and Red Lake participated in pageants at the popular "Chippewa Village," where Indigenous performers erected teepees and wigwams, paddled birch-bark canoes, held powwows, and occasionally reenacted battles with white performers. Performers could earn extra income posing for photographs; dramatic images that positioned Indigenous people in the past were especially popular with tourists. In a vintage 1930 Itasca postcard, a young handsome family with three children poses next to their fully packed travois, the mother beautifully attired in deerskin and the father in full headdress. For many decades, the Minnesota State Fair featured an "Indian Village," with its heyday in the 1930s. In 1935, the WPA sponsored a state fair powwow in St. Paul, and singers and dancers from White Earth exhibited their culture. Fairgoers, invited to view

Indigenous wild rice harvesting techniques, looked in on a live demonstration as an Ojibwe woman parched rice.[23]

Ojibwe workers incorporated emergency relief and conservation employment to their expanding repertoire of labor during the Great Depression. "An Indian family was never without meat or fruit as is now the case," lamented a St. Croix Ojibwe man who looked after his family during the Depression by finding work as a pulpwood cutter for the WPA and by sending his daughter to a government boarding school. Hundreds of Indian families across the United States sought out boarding schools for their children as a strategy of family preservation rather than a commitment to assimilation principles, making the 1930s the decade of highest student population in the once detested Indian schools. Recent decades of removals, land theft, violations to hunting, fishing, and gathering rights, and the wounds of assimilation left Ojibwe people with few resources to negotiate the 1930s. An anthropologist conducting fieldwork at White Earth in Minnesota during the Depression found that nearly all residents relied on some form of poverty relief or pension programs. More difficult to document were the cultural patterns of reciprocity, the deeply ingrained institutions of sharing, and the generosity of spirit that encouraged one to think of others—all of which had always sustained Ojibwe life through hard times, including the Great Depression.[24]

Ojibwe Labor during the Great Depression

In the 1930s, the depths of the Great Depression, state and federal officials began to search for local solutions to the poverty that overwhelmed Ojibwe Country. The Civilian Conservation Corps–Indian Division, an Indian New Deal program created by the federal government to provide work relief to Indian people, was active on nearly all the Minnesota reservations and communities. American Indians across the country had the option of joining family camps operated by the CCC–ID, but this program seems to have played a minor role for Indigenous families in the Great Lakes. The first CCC–ID camp on the Red Lake Reservation in northern Minnesota got under way November 15, 1933, a few months after the national program for American Indians. There, male employees of the CCC–ID worked on forest projects. They received a modest salary of thirty dollars a month before contributing a small sum for food and shelter, and most of their wages were sent to dependent relatives, as was also the case for white workers in the CCC. Workers who lived at home, as did many from Indigenous communities at Red Lake, White Earth, Lake Vermilion, and Grand Portage, could earn a monthly salary of forty-two dollars. Minneapolis was the Great Lakes regional headquarters for the program, which provided relief work to Ojibwes and Dakotas in Minnesota as well as Indians in Wisconsin and North Dakota. Men traveled considerable distances in northern Minnesota when work opportunities diminished closer to home. Families separated, and young men bunked for weeks at a time in emergency work camps. The Consolidated Chippewa Agency rotated men in and out of jobs to widen the pool of those participating in relief work.

The CCC–ID handbook makes some mention of the roles of women in poverty relief programs. For example, "Enrollee women serving as camp matrons will assist, also, in such recreation and leisure-time activity as will make camp life attractive." A small number of Ojibwe women found employment as social workers, investigating the problems of needy Indian families. Isabella Robideau held an influential position in Wisconsin and Minnesota, recommending men for hire in CCC–ID work camps and organizing financial arrangements for their dependents. Indian men wrote respectful letters to Robideau seeking her permission to enter work camps. Robideau's correspondence displays the confidence with which she meted out advice to camp foremen regarding intimate details of their employees' lives on matters including the distribution of men's salaries to their relatives, which meant parents and other adults as well as wives and children. In 1937,

Work crews departing Red Lake, about 1935. A federal employee took the photograph at Red Lake Agency; no other identifying information survives.

she wrote to the agency superintendent regarding the CCC–ID's practice of hiring white men married to Indian women. Indian men working for the Fond du Lac CCC–ID mobile unit near Cloquet, Minnesota, circulated a petition favoring the employment of a white World War I veteran who "attended council meetings faithfully," who drove a "ramshackled car that he takes seven men to work in," and who had married Kate Pequette, a Fond du Lac tribal member. Their correspondence suggests the fluidity of Ojibwe family life during the Great Depression, and the importance of kinship and contributing to the common good over foreign concepts of blood quantum. The veteran, his wife Kate, and their three tribally enrolled children were all "accepted as an Indian family" and valued as community members.[25]

John Collier, commissioner of Indian Affairs, wrote to the Consolidated Chippewa Agency in 1935 to emphasize that "married men with families" be given priority in hiring. Robideau explained to her agency colleagues that Ojibwe men would leave home only as a last resort. At a time when "county relief was slim and rather difficult to obtain," many Ojibwe had no alternative other than to join up to build roads, restore forests, or work on housing projects. Indian boarding school graduate Alphonse Caswell watched for forest fires as a WPA employee on the Red Lake Reservation. Ojibwe artist George Morrison, born on the north shore of Lake Superior near the Grand Portage Reservation, began work in the CCC–ID camp in Grand Portage along with young Indian men from across Minnesota, earning a monthly salary of thirty dollars. At the age of seventeen, Morrison labored in the kitchen and woods, doing "good healthy work" that encouraged community and friendship among the people assembled in the camps from a number of Ojibwe bands in the Great Lakes. They lived in barracks, dined communally, and played baseball. In the forests, they attacked the blight of blister rust, pulling diseased white pines out of the ground by their roots.[26]

Commissioner Collier argued for the involvement of "Indians themselves" in decision making for emergency conservation projects and envisioned cooperation between tribal councils, community members, managers, and CCC–ID superintendents. In a landscape designed by forest and water, where Indigenous people favored wild rice and maple sugar, projects in the Great Lakes were naturally shaped by Ojibwe experiences in the lake and woodland environment. One of the first efforts to promote and upgrade Ojibwe ricing took place near Lake Superior when a crew worked to restore the historic Grand Portage Trail, an important route once used by Indians and the Hudson's Bay Company. The trail was grown over with brush, and Grand Portage harvesters could not easily reach their rice lakes. Men working for the WPA and CCC–ID were still obligated to help their families move to seasonal work sites. The Nett Lake CCC–ID Camp, where the men planted trees to prevent soil erosion but also worked to improve water levels for wild rice, was located in Minnesota's premier wild rice region. The Nett Lake camp was virtually abandoned in August as workers left "for the wild rice fields"—even "overhead machine operators" walked off the job. Rather than refusing to go along with Ojibwe gathering in hard times, managers and superintendents became involved, deciding to take charge and improve the Indigenous harvest.[27]

White Men Discover Wild Rice

In the end, the good seed, still hand harvested by the world's leading experts, caught the attention of managers and government officials. Professors at the University of Minnesota had limited knowledge of the tall annual grain that grew naturally in the region's rivers and lakes. The authority on wild rice for the U.S. Department of Agriculture was Charles E. Chambliss, whose notions of the Indigenous harvest were hampered by his own cultural views and training. "The Indians of Minnesota, Wisconsin, and Canada, who use the seed of wild rice for food, harvest the grain in a very primitive way," wrote Chambliss in 1922. Though he would later change his mind, initially Chambliss failed to appreciate that Indigenous women were fine collective stewards of wild rice within the ecosystem of the Great Lakes, and he found their "primitive" methods of harvest incompatible with modern agricultural production. "Modernizing" the harvest could be accomplished, Chambliss reasoned, but only through the entry of non-Indian participants who would cultivate the wild grain, not just rely on natural processes, and who would employ machinery rather than obsolete knocking sticks to gather the rice.[28]

Chambliss's call to "modernize" the Ojibwe wild rice harvest in the 1920s bears some resemblance to earlier political rhetoric by those who sought to transform the division of labor in Indigenous agricultural societies based on their opposition to American gender roles. Indeed, politicians who favored Indian removal and allotment established their claims of Indian savagery on stereotypes of men as "indolent" and women as "drudges." Female Indigenous farmers with land rights had no place in the fantasies of U.S. reformers and politicians, and Indian boarding schools were charged with instilling an agenda that women were best suited to domesticity and only men were right for agriculture. The government officials during the Great Depression also based their notions of how to improve the Indigenous wild rice economy on American cultural standards, following in the footsteps of generations of policy makers who privileged male landownership and labor. The Ojibwe wild rice economy came into the spotlight during the Depression because of its potential to be "improved" and "modernized" through government management and the labor of men.

Wild rice production shifted rather abruptly into the hands of men soon after the government began to exert control over Indian ricing practices through the "modernization" programs of the WPA and CCC–ID. In Minnesota, the involvement of the state Forest Service furthered an increasingly male-centered project. Family and community rice camps where women collectively organized the harvest now contended with emergency conservation crews, whose managers promoted wild rice harvesting while simultaneously encouraging new methods and structures that emphasized male supervision and masculine industry.

The 1930s were a decade of radical change in wild rice production as the number of non-Indian harvesters and rice buyers multiplied and the first state regulations of ricing appeared. When the agronomist Chambliss returned to the upper Midwest during the summers of 1936 and 1938, he was appalled at the changes wrought by non-Indians who had recently entered the harvest: "During the past eight or ten years there has been a steady growth of whites entering the wild rice beds. They have been greedy and paid no attention to the natural laws regarding the plants['] reproduction. As a result many of the better wild rice beds have been ruined by whites gathering the crop in an immature state. The practice of the whites has forced the Indians to gather immature rice. This whole entire practice was ruining the wild rice in Minnesota."[29]

At White Earth, a large-scale project developed when the Minnesota State Forest Service set aside five acres of nontribal land near the Rice River as the "Indian Public Wild Rice Camp," cooperating with the Indian Service to oversee rice harvesting by permit. At Rice Lake, where the water level was controlled by a new dam built on the reservation, men were employed to construct "Indian rice camps" complete with modern conveniences. A report detailed the "modernized" camp scene at Rice Lake:

> Project Number One consists of a five acre camp, with five streets, six latrines, 1,600 feet of corduroy dock leading from the camp across the swampy land to the lake. It was found necessary to thin the dense stand of aspen and birch which covered the camp site, in order to provide space for Indian rice gathering and also for the rice gatherers to pitch their tents. Now the camp will enable at least two hundred Indians to harvest, thresh and transport many hundreds of thousands of pounds of wild rice. Every year thousands of dollars worth of wild rice is gathered by the Chippewas who come for many miles, for rice is an important winter food among the northern Indians. It is expected that the excellent facilities provided by such camps for rice gathering will enable the Chippewas to harvest the maximum amount.[30]

In the fall of 1934, fifteen hundred Ojibwe assembled at Rice Lake. For the first time in the visual documentation of Ojibwe wild ricing in the Great Lakes, the record shows a male harvest. In photographs, men in overalls are poling boats and knocking rice, while the Forest Service described the hulling operation as "a masculine affair." Women and children, now relegated to shore and camp, waited to parch the rice. Male work crews laid logs over swampy areas to ease the walk from camp and built canals along the docks to "enable harvesters to paddle their laden canoes as far inland as possible before transferring the wild rice to sacks which are then carried the rest of the way to the camps." Government officials celebrated the 1934 harvest in detailed reports to Washington, commenting on how the Ojibwe crew had excavated historic pottery from the site as they constructed canals. One Forest Service supervisor remarked on this as evidence that Indian wild rice harvests "had been practiced for centuries," though his observation would have seemed obvious to the Indigenous crew. The supervisor followed with a comment that betrays a breathtaking ignorance of recent Ojibwe history: "Extension Department at Consolidated Chippewa has made extensive studies of the wild rice crop with the idea in view of eventually developing this natural source of income to the Indians." The report was lavishly illustrated with photographs of the modern rice campgrounds, showing the impressive new "facilities." As a follow-up, the Cass Lake extension office advertised recipes for wild rice pudding, stuffing, and croquettes, since "within the past three years the State of Minnesota has realized the importance of wild rice to the Indians."[31]

The resurgence of the wild rice economy must have seemed ironic to Ojibwe workers who lived through the Great Depression, especially those who had witnessed the tragic destruction of that economy in previous decades. The establishment of emergency work camps had somehow roused government officials, especially the state Forest Service in Minnesota, to develop an appreciation for the older Indigenous economy it had, for the previous half century, meticulously lobbied, legislated, and labored to destroy. The Ojibwe seasonal round came back to life, now with federal and state endorsement and supervision, to meet the needs of the impoverished Ojibwe. In another ironic twist, at community meetings government officials showed films of white maple syrup harvesters from Vermont and spoke confidently of their plans to show Ojibwe men not only how to properly harvest wild rice but how to turn sap into maple sugar, since their handmade taps for trees were also regarded as primitive.[32]

This episode in Ojibwe history is more than just a regional story of how government officials began to reassess the natural resources of the Great Lakes during the Depression. It also demonstrates the continuation of a familiar theme. Earlier, the allotment policy had promoted an ideal of male agricultural labor and the field matron program and the entire Indian education

Grace Rogers and Joe Aitken harvesting wild rice near Walker, 1939.

policy of off-reservation boarding schools had promoted female domesticity. It seems efforts to transform Indigenous gender roles had faded by the 1930s. Historians often say the Great Depression and the political reforms of the Indian New Deal were a time when government officials collaborated with Indian communities across the nation to address the terrible problem of Indian poverty, and federally sponsored work programs were constructive efforts to rebuild trust with American Indians. But as wage labor and poverty relief work became a necessity for Ojibwe families, federal and state agencies united their authority to once again shape practices of Indigenous labor, especially in relation to gender. Government work programs of the Depression contained a lesser-known project of female domesticity.[33]

Ojibwe people witnessed the expansion of wild rice, to a greater degree than ever before, into the non-Indigenous world during the Great Depression. They faced pressures from the marketplace, competition from incompetent non-Indigenous harvesters, and the imposition of state regulation where a highly successful, environmentally sound Indigenous legal system already existed. These changes might have been world shattering for Ojibwe women. A single fact, men now harvesting wild rice, did not signify a bright future. Yet, historian Theda Perdue has warned of the perils of the declension argument, the idea that American Indian women's power and status always declined in the face of colonization, because "the non-Native world concerned men far more than women." For generations, Ojibwe women were empowered by their labor of harvesting wild rice. Water was a gendered space where women possessed property rights, and a wild rice camp was a female work site. Was there a shift in power relationships between Ojibwe men and women as large numbers of men entered the harvest? Did women continue to harvest wild rice in the 1930s and during World War II, when it was still an important part of the Ojibwe economy? Women and men appeared willing to modify elements of their work if they could sustain their families and preserve the essential values of cultural sovereignty that gave meaning to Ojibwe life.[34]

Women Workers and the Wild Rice Co-op

To trace the working lives and status of Ojibwe women after 1930, it is useful to evaluate their connections to a wild rice cooperative that operated in northern Minnesota, as well as their interest in ricing by permit when that became a state requirement in 1939. It appears that women retained a foothold in the wild rice economy during and after the Great Depression and that men's growing participation in the harvest did not signal the demise of women's involvement. Women workers were vital actors in a wild rice cooperative that operated at Cass Lake, a town on the Leech Lake Indian Reservation in northern Minnesota, from 1930 to 1944. The cooperative started up with funds from several places, including federal money that was part of emergency conservation work, Indian Reorganization Act resources targeted for tribal business development, and, in later years, a loan from the Minnesota Chippewa Tribe. The cooperative had elected officers and paid wages to harvesters who brought in wild rice. Members of the cooperative could vote and share in any dividends that resulted. The cooperative sold blueberries, maple sugar, and a whole range of crafted objects such as birch-bark baskets in addition to wild rice. Members of the cooperative were from the Leech Lake Reservation, but some were from the more distant White Earth Reservation. The manager of the cooperative, appointed by the tribal executive committee of the Minnesota Chippewa Tribe, was Paul LaRocque of Beaulieu, Minnesota, who also served as rice buyer. Ojibwe harvesters brought their finished wild rice to a central warehouse at Cass Lake, and the

Mrs. Fields at wild rice harvest, Nett Lake Indian Reservation, 1939.

cooperative paid out total amounts that varied annually from
$15,000 to $30,000 to purchase it.[35]

What BIA records remain from the wild rice cooperative at
Cass Lake indicate that Ojibwe women were active in the organization. Three women referred to by name in records, Mrs.
Kate Nelson, Mrs. Lovelace, and Mrs. Broker, and one other un-
named Ojibwe woman were important harvesters for the wild
rice cooperative in the late 1930s, and the co-op delivered barrels,
necessary for parching rice, to the four women at their homes.
The cooperative described the wild rice it sold to the public as
"parched, finished, and graded under careful and expert supervision," a testimonial to the practiced skills of its Ojibwe women
participants. An Ojibwe woman, Cecelia Rock, managed the cooperative during the early 1940s, perhaps because of the absence
of Ojibwe men during the war years. The cooperative was discontinued in the mid-forties, for reasons attributed to the decline
of tourism in northern Minnesota during World War II, but these
were also years when rice crops were reported as poor.[36]

One young Ojibwe, photographed in her jingle dress holding
a bag of rice labeled with a drum with feathers and the words
"Chippewa Indian Wild Rice," helped market wild rice for the
cooperative. Gedakaakoons, or Little Porcupine, sits in the cooperative's log warehouse in Cass Lake nestled among Ojibwe
handicrafts manufactured by women. She resembles one of her
Minnesota commercial contemporaries: the Land O'Lakes "Indian Maiden." Land O'Lakes, an agricultural cooperative established in Minneapolis–St. Paul in 1921, has used the image since
1928 on its dairy products. The Ojibwe wild rice cooperative may
have merely re-appropriated the Indian Maiden from the appro-
priators. That an Ojibwe wild rice cooperative employed an "Indian Maiden" in its own modest marketing campaign was not
a sign of the demise of Ojibwe women as active harvesters but
rather a creative adoption of an already popular image of Indian
womanhood.[37]

Women not only played a role in the wild rice cooperative at

Gedakaakoons, or Little Porcupine, poses for a publicity shot that was used by the Chippewa Indian Co-op Marketing Association at Cass Lake, about 1930.

Cass Lake; they continued to harvest wild rice with their families in other regions of the Great Lakes. In 1939, Minnesota harvesters were required to purchase ricing licenses. In that year,
Ojibwe women including Sophia Robideau, Mrs. Antoine Barry,
Della Blair, and Mrs. Mike Shobiash harvested rice at Portage
Lake and Perch Lake in central Minnesota, contending with
non-Indian harvesters who had picked rice that was too green
and a game warden who had forced Indians off the lakes. Even
so, Mrs. Shobiash reported an increase in her harvest over the
previous year when water levels were low, bringing in four hundred pounds of green rice. One White Earth woman who applied
for a license, Naomi Warren LaDue, complained of a long trip to
Bemidji to pay her fee to the game warden. It is difficult to get a
picture of the actual number of women who harvested with ricing
licenses, since "a license issued to the head of an Indian family
permitted all members of the family to harvest rice," unlike the
case for non-Indian applicants. Ricing licenses, male rice camps,
and government work programs of the 1930s profoundly influenced Ojibwe women's labor practices associated with the wild
rice harvest, but they did not undermine the foundation of Ojibwe
culture or the people's profound connection to manoomin.[38]

Beginning in the 1930s, a decade of extreme economic uncertainty, men joined women as active harvesters of wild rice,
moving into the gendered spaces where Ojibwe women sang
harvesting songs and labored together in support of their families and a rich community life. Non-Indigenous harvesters and
rice buyers multiplied, and the first state regulations of ricing appeared. In 1939, Minnesota issued 2,514 licenses to harvest wild
rice, a mere 993 going to Indigenous harvesters and their families. The harvest further transformed as commercial firms and
individual buyers entered the market, by first purchasing green
wild rice from Indigenous and non-Indigenous harvesters, then
mechanically processing the grain. The harvest was no longer
a predominantly female world. Once again, Indigenous women
adapted, preserving the fundamental structures of Ojibwe society

by working with the wild rice cooperative at Cass Lake and ricing by state permit when that became a requirement.[39]

My grandfather's knocking sticks have been a good lesson to me, a historian of Ojibwe ancestry, on the complexity of material culture and reading ethnographic objects. In this case, the knocking sticks offer an interpretation of Ojibwe labor history that is not so much an example of tradition but instead a story of Indigenous adaptability and survival. Growing up in a family where men harvested rice, I mistakenly believed men were always central to the harvest. My mother's stories about the Ojibwe work sites of her childhood—fish camp and the sugar bush, along with her own cherished remembrances of the Auginash family rice camp—contributed to my assumption, a process anthropologists describe as "upstreaming." I have now learned that the labor techniques and cultural practices of the wild rice harvest are more a legacy of our grandmothers.[40]

In Ojibwe communities today, the harvest has changed. Boats are seldom crafted by hand, parching and processing is by machine, often even by non-Indians, and we buy rice off the shelves of the reservation store. But knocking sticks are pretty much the same—like my grandfather's—hand carved, lightweight, cedar.

Wild rice remains my people's sacred food, but we worry it will disappear. In the United States and Canada today, wild rice is an endangered resource, still threatened by declining habitat. Tribes have new worries spurred by scientific and agricultural research on the wild rice genome at the University of Minnesota. Politicians in Minnesota, including the governor and state legislators from the Iron Range district, favor mining interests over the protection of our beloved wild rice and the water in which it grows. Even as the Minnesota Pollution Control Agency continues to recommend the necessity of a decades-long rule to protect wild rice from concentrations of sulfate in its waters, standards are not enforced. Sulfates are a pollutant produced from taconite mining, and they eventually create an environment in lakes that is lethal to our natural stands of wild rice.[41]

A family at rice camp, Nett Lake Indian Reservation, 1947.

Ojibwe people continue to cherish the wild rice that brought our ancestors into the western Great Lakes and Mississippi River region and find it difficult to imagine a future without it, even as we solemnly recognize that today Minnesota is one of the very last places in the country where genuine manoomin still grows wild and in abundance. For now, I give thanks for my new year's supply of wild rice, hand harvested by my cousins in northern Minnesota in September, our season to renew and celebrate the history of labor that constructed a sovereign homeland in the Great Lakes.

Acknowledgments

Aaniin!

When my mother was about to turn sixty, she wrote to me that one thing she had learned from me was to be proud of our Ojibwe background and family. It was a wonderful compliment. If that was the case, it was a mutual education, because Florence and other Red Lake people have always been exceptionally proud of our families and homeland. The pride my mother and grandparents possessed as Ojibwe people is what I have always aspired to teach my own thoughtful children, Frankie and Benay. Perhaps like my mother, I too have come to appreciate aspects of Ojibwe life through them. I wish Florence were here to see that Frankie is active in Ojibwe ceremonial life (though I think she always knew he would be) and that Benay Jeanette, like her great-grandmother, is a jingle dress dancer (as my mother always knew she would be). Miigwech, Frankie and Benay.

Florence would have been so proud to see this book in print, and I want to express my deep gratitude to the family members who helped me along the way. My cousin Gerald Auginash was ready to lend a hand during the writing of the chapters about our grandparents, and his memories and stories about Jeanette and Fred were sharp and insightful. "Augie," as he is called in the Indian community, is very proud of being a "Red Laker" and loved our grandma Jeanette. My brother, Brian, though I don't tell him enough, is one of the great heroes of our family for his commitment to us all. Miigwech, Gerald and Brian.

It is a privilege to have friends who are amazing writers and scholars, willing to listen and talk through the deep and complicated issues. Louise Erdrich has a seemingly endless capacity for

Brenda and Florence Child, Redby, Minnesota, September 1987.

insight and stories related to Ojibwe people and families. Louise, her wonderful daughters, and her entire extended family are exceptional people who make living in the Twin Cities feel like home. John Borrows shares my love of scholarship about Ojibwe people. He also likes a good road trip up north and is exceedingly generous with his time and ideas when he has visited Red Lake. Miigwech, Louise and John.

I wish to thank my colleagues with the patience to read through early drafts of chapters and make comments on my progress. They include Sarah Chambers, David Chang, Katherine Hayes, Jean O'Brien, Jeffrey Ostler, and Phillip Round. David, Jeani, and our fine graduate students who regularly take part in the American Indian Studies Workshop on Friday afternoons make the University of Minnesota an extraordinary place to do work in Indian history. I thank Akikwe Cornell, Kasey Keeler, Rose Miron, Juliana Hu Pegues, Katie Phillips, and Jimmy Sweet for their comments on this manuscript. Former students, now professors, have contributed their expertise, especially Karissa

White and Erik Redix. I am fortunate to work with remarkable undergraduate students at Minnesota and a long list of students who show up in the American Indian Studies Senior Seminar. They include Persia Erdrich, Ashley Fairbanks, and Chato Gonzalez. My colleagues in the Department of American Indian Studies, John Nichols and Brendan Fairbanks, never fail to offer me good advice about Ojibwe concepts and language. Miigwech!

There are not enough superlatives to express my admiration for the staff and scholars associated with the Minnesota Historical Society. At the press, Ann Regan is an editor with a great heart and integrity. Simply, she believes that we should tell the truth about Indian history in our region, a conviction she shares with her partner in life, Bruce White. Bruce generously helped me answer questions about the history of the Ojibwe at Mille Lacs. Brian Hosmer made fine comments to improve the manuscript. Shannon Pennefeather is an exceptional editor, and both she and Ann brought their own professionalism and magic to this book. Debbie Miller helped me locate information about marriage licensing in postwar Minnesota, and she never fails when I ask her unusual questions in the library. I also appreciate the consistently helpful staff at the regional branches of the National Archives in Chicago and Kansas City. Miigwech!

While working on *My Grandfather's Knocking Sticks* I became involved in a very worthy project—the writing of a new Red Lake constitution. My committee follows in the footsteps of people with this same assignment in earlier years, in 1918 and 1958, and we are profoundly aware of how seriously they took their responsibility. I am inspired by the fellowship and dedication of the Constitutional Reform Initiative Committee at Red Lake, whose members are Mike Beaulieu, Sheldon Brown, Tom Cain, Stephanie Cobenais, Lorena Cook, Pamela Johns, Annette Johnson, Jerry Loud, Keith Lussier, Pamela Pierce, Eugene Stillday, and Tharen Stillday. You give me hope for our future as a people. And finally, Sheldon, I forgive your grandfather for shooting my grandfather in 1934.

Notes

Notes to Introduction

1. Here I paraphrase historian Jeffrey Ostler, whose powerful comment, "We also need to be reminded that survival is not the same as freedom," is made in his introduction, "Colonialism, Agency, and Power," to *The Plains Sioux and U.S. Colonialism from Lewis and Clark to Wounded Knee*, 5. He suggests the significance of a key word we sometimes take for granted in the writing of Indian history, *colonialism*.

2. See also Hosmer, Harmon, and O'Neill, "Interwoven Economic Histories"; Hosmer, *American Indians in the Marketplace*; O'Neill, *Working the Navajo Way*; Raibmon, *Authentic Indians*; Bauer, *We Were All Like Migrant Workers Here*; Ostler, *The Plains Sioux and U.S. Colonialism*, 4–5.

3. Smith, *Decolonizing Methodologies*, 20.

4. Census of the Red Lake Indians of the Red Lake Agency, 1919 and 1930.

5. Letter from M. R. Baldwin, Commissioner, to the U.S. Secretary of the Interior, White Earth, Minnesota, February 26, 1896, National Archives, Record Group 75, Kansas City. The topic of this letter, though written at White Earth, was the eastern boundary of the Red Lake Reservation and the survey map recognized by the surveyor general's office in Minnesota, as well as Red Lake people's understandings of the names of various waterways in the region.

6. Letter from Agent Mercer to the U.S. Secretary of the Interior, E. A. Hitchcock, Walker, Minnesota, July 3, 1900; letter from Agent Mercer to the Commissioner of Indian Affairs, Leech Lake Agency, July 20, 1900, both National Archives, Record Group 75, Kansas City.

7. An exception is Tressa Berman's *Circle of Goods*, which is a study of the Fort Berthold economy.

Notes to Chapter 1

1. In an earlier book, *Boarding School Seasons*, I spelled my grandfather's name as *Nawajawan* in accordance with my mother's spelling of his name. In this one, I rely on the spelling used in the Allotment Roll of 1913.

2. This particular event was recalled by my cousin, Gerald Auginash: conversation on October 23, 2012.

3. Jack Nodinishkung Kechegwe Auginash's date of birth was 1862, and he was listed as a "mixed-blood" of Sandy Lake in Aitkin County. His father was John Joseph Kewetahgwonabe, and his mother was Kahduck. My grandfather's brother, John Auginash, eventually had a large family at White Earth, and Grandpa's nieces and nephews were Joe (1922), Susan (1925), Norman (1927), Dorothy (1929), George (1931), and Isabelle (1933).

As I write, George is the only living Auginaush sibling, and he mentioned to me his childhood visits to Redby to see his uncle Fred, visits that were especially memorable to him because his own father died young when George was a very small child. These Auginaush siblings were also Ojibwe speakers, and stories by Joe Auginaush (1922–2000) appear in a book edited by Anton Treuer, *Living Our Language*, 152–63.

4. This has been brilliantly written about by Bruce White in an unpublished paper, "Criminalizing the Seasonal Round."

5. In 1850, a census taken in Minnesota Territory recorded the non-Indian population as quite small, listing just six thousand people in the nine counties. American Indians were 84 percent of the total population, a trend that would be reversed in the following decade.

6. Borrows, *Recovering Canada;* McClurken, et al., *Fish in the Lakes*, 514–24.

7. *Minnesota v. Mille Lacs Band of Chippewa Indians;* the opinion was delivered on March 24, 1999, written by Justice Sandra Day O'Connor.

8. McClurken, et al., *Fish in the Lakes*, 383.

9. McClurken, et al., *Fish in the Lakes*, 384.

10. For example, the 1855 Treaty of Washington led to the establishment of northern Minnesota reservations, and the White Earth Reservation was established by treaty in 1867. Nelson Act, 51st Congress, 1st Session, Ex. Doc. 247 (1889).

11. McClurken, et al., *Fish in the Lakes*, 391.

12. The Isle families were Nequenaby's band of Ojibwe. The Mille Lacs Ojibwe carefully responded to this and other outrageous acts of terror and encroachment on their lands with civility and legal suits, including letters to the secretary of the interior. James M. McClurken, "The Effect of Treaties and Agreements since 1855," in *Fish in the Lakes*, 422. Some Ojibwe people on the roll of 1913 are listed by an Ojibwe name, while others by an English name. Sometimes individuals are listed by both an Ojibwe and an English name. See *Roll of the Chippewa Indians Allotted Within the White Earth Reservation in the State of Minnesota*, prepared by the commission appointed under the Act of June 30th, AD 1913, Minnesota Historical Society.

13. The infamous Surveys of Indian Industry were conducted on reservations throughout the United States in the 1920s.

14. This name appears on official enrollment documents but was not her only Ojibwe name.

15. Jeanette Jones Auginash File, Records of the Red Lake Agency, Redlake, MN.

16. These and other direct quotations from my mother, Florence L. Auginash Child, are from a journal she wrote and gave to me as a Christmas present in 1997. She passed away in March 2001.

17. Fred, as I mentioned in the text, was actually forty-one. The letter was dated December 12, 1929.

18. The letters and marriage certificate were filed under my grandparents' names, Jeanette Auginash and Fred Auginash, in the tribal offices of the Red Lake Band of Chippewa, Red Lake, MN.

19. Fred Auginash File, Records of the Red Lake Agency.

20. Grant of Standard Assignment and Red Lake Agency Records, October 18, 1943, and January 29, 1944.

21. Jeanette Auginash File.

22. Fred Auginash File.

23. For unknown reasons, we always celebrated my mother's birthday on August 25, despite the accuracy, or not, of her birth certificate.

24. Red Lake Constitution; a published copy is accessible in the compilation by David E. Wilkins, *Documents of Native American Political Development*, 408–9.

25. Bureau of Indian Affairs (hereafter, BIA), Red Lake Agency, Records of the Red Lake Fisheries Association, National Archives, Record Group 75, Kansas City. This comment was made by the tribe's excellent

attorney in Detroit Lakes, Fred Dennis, in a letter dated February 28, 1938.

26. Conversation with Gerald Auginash, October, 23, 2012. This David Jones was Jeanette's cousin, not her father with the same name.

27. Florence Child Journal, 1997.

28. I came across these in Red Lake in August 2013, just as I was about to write about my grandfather.

29. All the letters in this section are from the Fred Auginash File.

30. Since this event, Daniel Needham has had the gratitude of the entire Auginash family. I interviewed him briefly when he was in his nineties; he attended Carlisle, and his experience in the outing program is referenced in *Boarding School Seasons*. After my son, Frankie, was born in 1989, my cousin Darrell Auginash gave him an Indian name, the same as Dan Needham's, Ombegeshig. During the ceremony he mentioned Daniel Needham had once saved our grandfather's life.

31. My cousin Gerald Auginash remembers that Joe Brown also lived in Copper City, within a quarter mile of Green Lake, saying "He was a tough old guy."

32. For the Anishinaabeg, one might have more than a single spiritual name during one's lifetime. These are quotations from Florence Child's journal, 1997.

Notes to Chapter 2

1. Certificate of Baptism, Gerald Robert Auginash, April 25, 1954.

2. Personal conversation with Gerald Auginash.

3. The Ojibwe name is a reference to the calf of a buffalo. These quotations and memories are from Florence Child's journal, 1997.

4. Dotis Imogene Auginash's Certificate of Death lists her date of death as July 1, 1943. Letter from the Red Lake Agency to the Ration Board in Bemidji, MN, July 19, 1943.

5. Letter of March 11, 1939, to Jeanette Auginash from the Beltrami County Welfare Board; Letter of June 27, 1940, to Mrs. David Jones from John H. Hougen, Tribal Attorney, Minnesota Chippewa Tribe.

6. A copy of the 1950s interview is held in the Red Lake Tribal Archives. Liebling and Liebling, "A Visit to Red Lake."

7. Liebling and Liebling, "A Visit to Red Lake," and Mittleholtz, "Historical Review."

8. Letter from Peter Graves to Mr. John H. Hougen, Redby, MN, August 9, 1940.

9. Letter from Superintendent Raymond H. Bitney, Red Lake Agency, to Mr. John H. Hougen, Tribal Attorney, August 12, 1940.

10. Indian Claims Commission reports estimated the Red Lake population as 1,881 in 1932 and 2,836 in 1950. My father told me of Peter Graves's friendly visits to the Auginash home, and the black car he drove. Mittleholtz, "Historical Review," 111.

11. The spelling of Frank Gurneau's name in official Red Lake documents is sometimes "Gurno."

12. Transcript of the hearing of Jeanette Auginash, Red Lake Court of Indian Offences, September, 5, 1942.

13. Florence Child Journal.

14. According to Edwin Mittleholtz, the non-Indians were 70 percent of the sawmill's work force in early decades of operation.

15. Letter to James R. Mitchell, Executive Secretary, Beltrami County Welfare Board, from Red Lake Indian Agency, April 1, 1948.

16. Minnesota State Board of Control-MPA-ADC Form 12, in the matter of the application of Fred Auginash, July 6, 1948.

17. Letter to Fred Auginash, Redby, MN, from Beltrami County Welfare Board, July 1, 1948.

18. Informal Notes of the Red Lake Agency, July 6–August 9, 1948.

19. Statement of Fred Auginash and Jeanette Auginash, Redby, MN, July 8, 1948, to Mr. Peru Farver, Superintendent, Red Lake Agency.

20. Notes from the Red Lake Indian Agency, August, 8, 1948.

21. Florence Child Journal, 1997. This petition is indicated in a series of letters to and from the Red Lake Agency in 1949 and 1950, in correspondence with the Family Allowance Division of the Army Finance Center, Office of the Chief of Finance, St. Louis, MO. Letter from Superintendent Peru Farver, Red Lake Indian Agency, August 23, 1949.

22. Letter from Superintendent Peru Farver, Red Lake Indian Agency, April 27, 1950.

23. Action of the Red Lake Band of Chippewa Indians, Resolution No. 2, Serial 1099, Approval of Petition for Adoption of Gerald Smith by Jeanette Auginash, August 7, 1957.

24. Translation courtesy of Brendan Fairbanks.

25. Frustrating to me, the date on the postcard is illegible, and the three-cent stamp on the card was common on letters beginning in 1938

and through the 1950s. It was probably mailed February 1, 1952. It has a desert picture on the front, "Rodeo Time." This card would not place Vernon in northern Minnesota in the winter of 1952, as my mother suggested, so perhaps they met the following early winter of December 1952. Florence Child's journal, 1996.

26. At the time of my father's letter in March 1953, his sister Connie was a recently married young professional just beginning a long career as a secretary with John Deere and Company in Moline, Illinois. The letter makes reference to her husband, Jerry Finch, as well as his brother's wife, Shirley. Dick and Shirley Child were residents of Matherville, Illinois, the town where my father grew up.

27. Author's personal collection.

28. This was in the wake of the famous black prizefighter Jack Johnson's relationships with and subsequent marriages to white women in Chicago in 1911 and 1912. Historian Peggy Pascoe has written a comprehensive study of the presence of miscegenation laws in the United States, which were continuously enforced in various regions and states until they were declared unconstitutional by the U.S. Supreme Court in the 1967 *Loving* decision. See Pascoe, *What Comes Naturally* (quote 8–9).

29. Regarding marriage licenses, this appears to be a consistent practice across Minnesota counties. For example, applications for marriage licenses in Martin County in 1931 do not ask for information about race, and neither do applications in Wadena County in 1952. Minnesota Statutes 1945, Section 517.02. The judge was Marcus Reed, and the other witness was Andrew Gronseth, a name not familiar to me. It appears he died in Beltrami County in 1963.

30. *Roll of the Chippewa Indians Allotted Within the White Earth Reservation*. The settlement valued land at the time of taking, rather than at current prices.

31. Letter from H. Kleinman, MD, Senior Physician, Red Lake Indian Hospital, August 28, 1951. The letter was copied to the Veterans Service Officer in Bemidji and the Superintendent of the Red Lake Agency, Frell. M. Owl, as well as Fred Auginash.

32. Notes from the Red Lake Agency dated August 8, 1956–October 27, 1957.

33. Conversation with Gerald Auginash, October 2012.

34. Florence Child Journal, 1996.

35. In the 1960s and 1970s, Housing and Urban Development structures dominated reservation architecture.

Notes to Chapter 3

1. Letter to A. C. Klancke, Supervisor, Bureau of Commercial Fishing, State Game and Fish Department, June 27, 1929.

2. Eastman, "Life and Handicrafts of the Northern Ojibwas."

3. Eastman, "Life and Handicrafts of the Northern Ojibwas."

4. Eastman, *Indian Boyhood*, 1.

5. Eastman, "Life and Handicrafts of the Northern Ojibwas"; Densmore, *Chippewa Customs*, 124–27.

6. For a discussion of more contemporary issues related to Red Lake fishing, see the documentary film *Return of the Red Lake Walleye* (Native Nations Institute for Leadership, Management, and Policy, Udall Center for Public Policy, University of Arizona, 2012). Christian W. McMillen reconstructs the history of land survey corruption and its role in Indian dispossession in a fascinating study about a case that went to the U.S. Supreme Court and that would revolutionize issues of aboriginal title. See *Making Indian Law*.

7. Red Lake Chippewa Constitution, adopted April 13, 1918.

8. Bruce White discussed the photographer Roland Reed at Red Lake in his book *We Are at Home*, 146–56.

9. Six of the seven hereditary chiefs, who ranged in age from their early thirties to Medweganoonind in his eighties, signed the Agreement of 1889.

10. "Chippewa Indians in Minnesota," 51st Congress, 1st Session, House Executive Documents, no. 247—serial 2747 (1889). The report of the commissioners is dated December 26, 1889, and is referred to as the Rice Report.

11. Agreement with the Red Lake Band of Chippewa Indians, Act of January 14, 1889, 25 Stat., 642–46.

12. Partial letter written to Commissioner of Indian Affairs Thomas J. Morgan, Brainerd, MN, August 5, 1889, National Archives, Record Group 75, Kansas City.

13. Letters from the Leech Lake Agency, Walker, MN, June 12, 1899.

14. Minnesota governor John Lind. The commission lasted from

1917 to 1919. Minnesota Commission of Public Safety files, Minnesota Historical Society.

15. Conversation with John D. Nichols, July 30, 2013.

16. S. A. Selvog, "State Fisheries Activities During 1925."

17. Hagg, "Logging Line."

18. Minnesota State Fisheries Game and Fish Department, Redby, MN, January 10, 1925, National Archives, Record Group 75, Kansas City; Hagg, "Logging Line," 132. Contract negotiated on January 25, 1924, in St. Paul, MN.

19. Letter of Superintendent S. A. Selvog, June 10, 1925, Minnesota State Fisheries Game and Fish Department, National Archives, Kansas City.

20. Report of January 25, 1924, BIA, National Archives, Kansas City.

21. Letter from A. C. Kvennes, Middle River, MN, to Red Lake Agency, December 31, 1925; letter from Commissioner of Minnesota State Game and Fish Department, September 14, 1926, both BIA, National Archives, Kansas City.

22. Letter from Assistant Commissioner E. B. Merritt, July 1, 1925, BIA, National Archives, Kansas City newspaper clipping included with letter of May 27, 1925, BIA, National Archives, Kansas City; letter from S. A. Selvog to Minnesota State Fisheries Game and Fish Department, February 21, 1925.

23. Letter from State of Minnesota Game and Fish Commission, February 11, 1925, BIA, National Archives, Kansas City.

24. Selvog, "State Fisheries Activities During 1925," emphasis in original; report to the Interim Commission of the Minnesota State Legislature by James F. Gould, State Game and Fish Commission, Old Capitol, St. Paul, MN, BIA, National Archives, Kansas City.

25. Letter from Commissioner of Indian Affairs to the Red Lake Agency, April 24, 1926, BIA, National Archives, Kansas City.

26. The number of fisher men and women varied from 210 in 1924 to 156 the following year, probably due to the quantity of nets and equipment available.

27. Letter from Edward L. Rogers to James F. Gould, Game and Fish Commissioner, September 27, 1926; letter from James F. Gould, Game and Fish Commissioner, to Mr. Edward L. Rogers, September 28, 1926, both BIA, National Archives, Kansas City.

28. Letter to James F. Gould, Commissioner of Game and Fish, from

Mark L. Burns, Red Lake Agency, October 13, 1926, BIA, National Archives, Kansas City.

29. Letter to James F. Gould, Commissioner of Game and Fish, from Mark L. Burns, Red Lake Agency, October 25, 1926; letter of Commissioner of Indian Affairs Charles H. Burke to James F. Gould, October 26, 1926, both BIA, National Archives, Kansas City.

30. Commissioner Gould cited General Statute 1923 and provisions section 5604 to 5609 in his letter to Commissioner Burke. Burke to Gould, October 26, 1926; letter of S. A. Selvog, Minnesota State Fisheries to Mark L. Burns, Red Lake Agency, July 16, 1926, BIA, National Archives, Kansas City.

31. David Wilkins considers Red Lake as among the sixty tribal nations to adopt constitutions prior to 1934, after which another one hundred thirty underwent the process. Wilkins believes that many of the early constitutions reflected community goals. See his *Documents of Native American Political Development;* also see Vizenor and Doerfler, *The White Earth Nation.*

32. Letter to Edward L Rogers from Peter Graves, Redby, MN, January 13, 1927, BIA, National Archives, Kansas City.

33. Letter of James F. Gould to Mark L. Burns, March 23, 1927, BIA, National Archives, Kansas City.

34. Letter of Commissioner of Indian Affairs Charles H. Burke to James F. Gould, January 19, 1926, BIA, National Archives, Kansas City.

35. Burke to Gould, January 19, 1926; letter of Commissioner of Game and Fish James Gould to Harold Knutson, Member of Congress, February 16, 1927, BIA, National Archives, Kansas City.

36. Gould to Knutson, February 16, 1927; State of Minnesota, 46th Session, H.F. No. 540, February 15, 1929.

37. The suit was brought by M. W. Lipinski, a fish wholesale dealer from Winona.

38. Letter to George McCullough, Commissioner of Game and Fish, from Dennis and Bell, Detroit Lakes, January 29, 1929; letter to Mark L. Burns from Howard K. Baech, January 28, 1929, both BIA, National Archives, Kansas City.

39. Letter to Commissioner of Indian Affairs from Red Lake Attorneys Dennis and Bell, February 19, 1929, BIA, National Archives, Kansas City.

40. Proceedings of the General Council of the Red Lake Band of Chippewa Indians, March 1, 1929, BIA, National Archives, Kansas City.

41. Letter to Mark L. Burns from Commissioner Charles Burke, Office of Indian Affairs, Washington, DC, May 25, 1929; letter to Mark L. Burns from David Brassard, Walker, MN, May 8, 1929, both BIA, National Archives, Kansas City.

42. Letter to A. C. Klancke, Supervisor, Bureau of Commercial Fishing, State Game and Fish Department, June 27, 1929.

43. Letter to Mark L. Burns from Dennis and Bell, July 18, 1929, BIA, National Archives, Kansas City.

44. Letter to Governor Harold Stassen from Fred Dennis, Detroit Lakes, MN, January 24, 1939, BIA, National Archives, Kansas City.

45. Letter to the Commissioner of Indian Affairs from Fred Dennis, January 26, 1939, BIA, National Archives, Kansas City.

46. Letter from Raymond H. Bitney to Peter Graves, Red Lake Band of Chippewa Indians General Council, February 2, 1939, BIA, National Archives, Kansas City.

47. Letter to Harry E. Speakes from Peter Graves, Red Lake, MN, May 11, 1939, BIA, National Archives, Kansas City.

48. Letter to Raymond H. Bitney from Fred Dennis, Detroit Lakes, MN, May 11, 1939, BIA, National Archives, Kansas City. This comment was made by the tribe's excellent attorney in Detroit Lakes, Fred Dennis, in a letter dated February 28, 1938.

49. Records of the Red Lake Fisheries Association, BIA, Red Lake Agency, National Archives, Record Group 75, Kansas City.

50. Probably "dragging the river" was for logging purposes. Letter from Max Jones to Superintendent Raymond Bitney, Warroad, MN, April 6, 1939, BIA, Records of the Red Lake Agency, National Archives, Record Group 75, Kansas City.

51. See also Child, *Holding Our World Together*.

Notes to Chapter 4

1. We now celebrate Chief's Day on July 6 in recognition of our hereditary leaders who negotiated the Agreement of 1889.

2. This point was made by Raymond D. Fogelson in his classic essay, "The Ethnohistory of Events and Nonevents," *Ethnohistory* 36.2 (spring 1989): 133–47.

3. Compare this to the 12,400 estimated deaths from H1N1 in the United States.

4. While the American Indian population steadily climbed throughout the twentieth century, an exception was the 1918–19 period.

5. The story is repeated at powwows at Red Lake, and especially at times when a drum group from Fort Berthold is in attendance.

6. As in Alfred Crosby, *America's Forgotten Pandemic: The Influenza of 1918*. There is remarkably little scholarly literature on the Jingle Dress Dance. Tara Browner's book *Heartbeat of the People* discusses the dance in some detail, but other recent studies of the powwow only mention it in passing.

7. Young girls and women also sought visions, like their male counterparts, even though spiritual power came to them at menarche. Nineteenth-century narratives about Bear Woman of Leech Lake and Catherine Waboose, who told her story to Ojibwe writer Jane Johnston Schoolcraft, emphasize the seclusion, fasting, and visions experienced by young Ojibwe women during coming-of-age rituals. Child, *Holding Our World Together*, 1–8.

8. Many scholars have discussed the controversial Dance Order. For example, Hoxie, *A Final Promise*, and Kelly, *The Assault on Assimilation*. Troutman, *Indian Blues*, 2, 4.

9. Commissioner of Indian Affairs Charles Burke issued a government circular, "Indian Dancing," in 1921. Troutman, *Indian Blues*, 13, 20.

10. See Witgen, *An Infinity of Nations*.

11. This idea is discussed by ethnomusicologist Thomas Vennum in "The Ojibway Begging Dance."

12. Thanks to Marcia Anderson, curator at the Minnesota Historical Society, for showing me jingle dresses in the collection.

13. Vennum, *The Ojibwa Dance Drum*.

14. I appreciate the assistance of Professor Patricia Albers for this lesson in dating postcards, as well as providing me access to her extensive collection of American Indian postcards, which focuses on images of Native people of the Great Lakes and northern plains.

15. Marquette University archivist Mark Thiel agrees with my contention that the Jingle Dress Dance emerged around the time of the Spanish influenza, having observed the same patterns in women's regalia in photographs from the Marquette collections. See his short essay, "Origins of the Jingle Dress Dance."

16. Albers and Medicine, "Some Reflections," 26; Browner, *Heartbeat of the People*, 53.

17. Albers and Medicine, "Some Reflections," 40. "Prayer of healing" is Tara Browner's phrase. Browner also mentions that other tribal groups, the Lakota and Ho-Chunk in particular, have developed renditions of jingle dress origin stories that incorporate their own tribes in the telling.

18. Young, "Recent Health Trends"; Joe and Young, eds., *Diabetes: A Disease of Civilization*.

19. Child, *Boarding School Seasons*.

20. BIA, National Archives, Record Group 75, Chicago.

21. BIA, National Archives, Record Group 75, Chicago.

22. For example, Katherine Osburn, *Southern Ute Women*. Josephine Bonga is listed as "housekeeper" in the Funds and Property of the Chippewa Indians of Minnesota, 62nd Congress, 2nd Session, House of Representatives, March 22, 1912.

23. Babcock and Parezo, *Daughters of the Desert*. Densmore's trip to Grand Portage is described by Nancy L. Woolworth in "Miss Densmore Meets The Ojibwe."

24. Densmore, "Chippewa Music" and "Chippewa Music II."

25. Foreword to "Chippewa Music" and "Chippewa Music II," 1013.

26. Densmore wrote a biographical sketch of Julia Spears Warren and made this point about the naming of Madeline Island: Densmore Papers, Minnesota Historical Society. Of course, Ojibwe people had long referred to Madeline Island as Mooniingwanenaning, and it is the heart of the Ojibwe homelands in the Great Lakes.

William W. Warren had a short life of twenty-eight years (1825–53) but wrote a classic study published as "The History of the Ojibwe People" in 1885 by the Minnesota Historical Society as volume 5 of the *Collections of the Minnesota Historical Society*. The book is still in print as *The History of the Ojibway People*.

27. This information comes from Densmore's biographical sketch of Julia Spears Warren. Densmore mentioned the tribal celebration held at White Earth on June 14, 1907. The White Earth Pow Wow is still held on this date every year.

This passage was taken from Densmore's typed introduction of "Prelude to the Study of Indian Music in Minnesota," in the Densmore Papers.

28. Lieberman, "A Review of the Effectiveness of *Cimicifuga Racemosa.*

29. Densmore, "Uses of Plants," "Beverages" section, 317–18.

30. Densmore, "Uses of Plants," 297.

31. Densmore, "Uses of Plants," 322.

32. Densmore, *Chippewa Customs,* 128. Densmore's study was first published in 1929 by the Smithsonian Institution Bureau of American Ethnology, "Annual Report," Bulletin 86.

33. "Uses of Plants," "Making Maple Sugar" section, 308–13.

34. "Uses of Plants," 309.

35. "Uses of Plants, 313.

36. "Uses of Plants," "Surgical Treatment and Appliances" section, 332–35; typescript of presentation, WCCO Radio, March 9, 1932, in Densmore Papers.

37. For an excellent intellectual history of the assimilation policy, see Hoxie, *A Final Promise.* For a history of government boarding schools that emphasizes Ojibwe people, see Child, *Boarding School Seasons.* Neihardt, *Black Elk Speaks;* La Farge, *Laughing Boy.*

38. The World Indigenous Peoples Conferences include presentations on Indigenous plants and medicines as part of the program. The meetings attract Indigenous Peoples from around the globe, including Native Canadians, Native Americans and Hawaiians, Aboriginal Australians, the Maori from New Zealand, and other Pacific Islanders.

39. "The Deadly Virus: The Influenza Epidemic of 1918: Selected Records from the National Archives," available: http://www.archives. gov/exhibits/influenza-epidemic/records-list.html.

Notes to Chapter 5

1. Constance Arzigian writes that wild rice appears in sites in southern Wisconsin dating from AD 100–200, though it was a more important part of the economy in northern Wisconsin and Minnesota and harvested by Indigenous people for "at least a thousand years." Arzigian, "Middle Woodland and Oneota Contexts," 245, 262–63.

2. In 1940, a biologist for the Soil Conservation Service of the USDA wrote from Baudette, Minnesota, to colleagues in Minneapolis to discuss the issue of game protection along the northern border of the Red Lake Reservation, referring in particular to woodland caribou.

Minneapolis Area Office, Series 508793, Box 25, National Archives, Record Group 75, Kansas City.

3. The Ojibwe homeland is the Great Lakes region of the United States and Canada, though historians seldom cross the border in their writing. Some Ojibwe writers have transcended the border, including Basil Johnston and Gerald Vizenor. My own study emphasizes U.S. federal policy and Ojibwe labor history in Wisconsin and Minnesota. Of course, Ojibwe in Canada also harvest wild rice and have a rich labor history.

4. Anthropologist Stuart Berde's fieldwork in northern Minnesota during the 1965 ricing season is typical of scholarly studies that emphasize wild rice as gender-neutral labor, though his study reflects Ojibwe ricing practices of that period: "Although both men and women gather rice, the division of labor is not strictly by sex; rather, it is based on the experience of the ricing pair." Berde, "Wild Ricing," 105.

Indigenous harvester James Mustache, Sr., commented that Ojibwe men began to harvest wild rice in the 1930s. His view included the statement, "Never see any women now." Vennum, *Wild Rice and the Ojibway*, 109–10.

5. Most historians describe wild rice labor as shared by men and women. Hosmer, *American Indians in the Marketplace*, 22.

6. The painting is in the Longworth House Office building. Colette Hyman viewed Dakota labor in the wild rice harvest as a shared responsibility, writing that "Dakota women and men worked together to harvest psin" in her book *Dakota Women's Work*, 22. Mary Henderson Eastman shared the biased views of many of her contemporaries about Dakota society and women but had a strange fascination with Dakota love stories, perhaps a result of her husband's prior relationship with a Dakota woman. Eastman, *Dahcotah*.

7. Scholars have suggested wild rice increased in importance to Ojibwe people after the decline of the fur trade in the early nineteenth century. Hickerson, *The Chippewa and Their Neighbors*; Peers, *The Ojibwa of Western Canada*.

Catlin, *Letters and Notes*; Thwaites, ed., "Radisson and Groseilliers in Wisconsin"; Lawrence Taliaferro to Samuel Pond, August 26, 1939, Samuel Pond Papers, Minnesota Historical Society. Taliaferro had a short-term relationship with Anpetu Inajinwin, a Dakota woman who was the mother of the eleven-year-old daughter he writes about in this letter to missionary Samuel Pond. His daughter lived at Lake Calhoun, which is why she must "leave the Lake" to harvest rice at another location. An article about the Dakota daughters of early Anglo men in Minnesota is Jane Lamm Carroll, "Who Was Jane Lamont?" Jenks, "The Wild Rice Gatherers."

8. Frances Densmore, "Chippewa Customs," *Bureau of American Ethnology* 86 (1929): 128. Chambliss was in charge of rice investigations for the USDA and favored a scientific approach to wild rice cultivation by non-Indians. At his Arlington, Virginia, experimental farm "almost perfect stands of wild rice have been obtained" of the broad-leafed species *Zizania palustris*, related to the *Zizania aquatica* that grows in the Great Lakes. Chambliss regarded Indigenous methods of tending and harvesting wild rice as "simple," saying the Ojibwe harvested "the grain in a very primitive way." See Chambliss, "Wild Rice," 13.

The largest scholarly influence on my ideas about wild rice is Thomas Vennum's *Wild Rice and the Ojibway.* Indeed, it was difficult to locate sources about the history of wild rice that Vennum had not already considered. Vennum appreciated that wild rice was historically women's labor, but his own work drew on the information provided by harvesters he spoke with during the 1970s and 1980s, when it was a predominantly male endeavor. What I have attempted to add to the labor history of wild rice is the topic of gender. Vennum, *Wild Rice and the Ojibway,* 82.

9. William Warren was born in 1825, the descendent of fur traders and the Ojibwe hereditary chief White Crane. He died at age twenty-eight, after completing a remarkable manuscript based on Ojibwe oral history that was published after his death. Warren mentioned that for Ojibwe women, "Their hard work, however, again commences in the autumn, when the wild rice which abounds in many of the northern inland lakes, becomes ripe and fit to gather. Then, for a month or more, they are busied in laying in their winter's supply." There is reason to believe that Warren was very familiar with the Ojibwe seasonal round, and he reportedly manufactured a thousand pounds of maple sugar in 1852, the year before his premature death. Warren, *History of the Ojibway,* 186, 266.

Kegg paid tribute to her resourceful mentor in a book transcribed and edited by linguist John D. Nichols: *Maude Kegg,* 124–25.

10. One of Densmore's informants, Nodinens from Mille Lacs,

described the work of harvesting maple sugar as women's labor: "When we got to the sugar bush we took the birch-bark dishes out of the storage and the women began tapping the trees." Regarding men's labor, she remarked, "Our sugar camp was always near Mille Lac, and the men cut holes in the ice, put something over their heads, and fished through the ice." Densmore, *Chippewa Customs*, 122. Rogers, *Red World and White*, 26.

11. According to Coleman's 1929 fieldwork, "The main function of this procedure, according to a few informants, was to keep the kernels from the birds, but it seemed generally agreed that in any case it indicated property rights." Coleman, "The Ojibwa and the Wild Rice Problem"; Densmore, "Uses of Plants," 313. Hosmer also suggests Menominee women held usufruct rights to maple sugar groves. Hosmer, *American Indians in the Marketplace*, 22–23.

12. Vennum has an insightful discussion of the importance of binding rice and ways in which the practice changed over the years among Ojibwe communities. See Vennum, *Wild Rice and the Ojibway*, 82–90. Vennum relied on Robert Ritzenthaler's field notes, and he found only two women on the Lac Courte Oreilles Reservation who still practiced binding in 1941. *Wild Rice and the Ojibway*, 90. Ritzenthaler simply suggests that binding may have discontinued because it "meant extra work." Ritzenthaler and Ritzenthaler, *The Woodland Indians of the Western Great Lakes*, 25.

13. Maude Kegg used the term *oashkaabewisag* to refer to the ricing officials from Mille Lacs in Minnesota. *Oshkaabewisag* is the plural of a term that translates as ceremonial attendant or messenger. Kegg, *Portage Lake*, 122–23. Brian Hosmer mentions that the Menominee delegated a similar role to the warrior society, or mitewuk. Hosmer, *American Indians in the Marketplace*, 22. See also Nichols and Nyholm, *A Concise Dictionary of Minnesota Ojibwe.*

Vennum mentions that Nett Lake Ojibwe remembered all-male ricing committees during the 1940s, though women could be members. Ricing chiefs oversaw the committee selection process every spring. Vennum, *Wild Rice and the Ojibway*, 180–81.

During Clark's childhood in the 1930s, he recalled his "parents" riced. Clark, *Naawigiizis*, 62–64.

14. Daniel Stanchfield, a lumberman from Maine in Minnesota in 1847, commented, "When we came to the Rice lakes, eight miles from

Mille Lacs, the squaws had tied the rice together for threshing, and therefore the canoe could not pass through and had to be taken to the shore." For over six miles, Stanchfield observed the wild rice gatherers. See Stanchfield, "History of Lumbering," 331–32.

15. Albers, "Labor and Exchange in American Indian History," 277. Work that considers American Indian labor history and gender includes Littlefield and Knack, *Native Americans and Wage Labor;* O'Neill, *Working the Navajo Way;* Berman, *Circle of Goods;* Raibmon, *Authentic Indians.*

One early Minnesota lumberman who kept a diary commented on women's wild rice labor. "When it is ripe the squaws will take their canoes and padle roiund [sic] among it. They cut the head off with knives. It is some like oats. They then will dry it and put it on a blanket and tred [sic] it out with their feet. They then put it in a barrel and pound the hull off from it with sharp sticks. The squaws do [sic] all the work and the bucks hunt a little." His comments are typical of western observers of Indian life in North America, who characteristically derided Indian men's labor as inadequate and viewed all Indigenous people as "indolent," even while being supplied by Natives for many of their basic needs. Lumberman's Diary, June 12, 1855, Ms A-L 958, Minnesota Historical Society.

16. White, "Criminalizing the Seasonal Round." Frederick Hoxie also discussed how squatters on the Mille Lacs Reservation were able to have claims to Indian land entered in the local land office, while Ojibwe landowners were turned away if they attempted to register a claim. See Bruce White, "Ojibwe-White Conflicts over Land and Resources on the Mille Lacs Reservation, 1855–1923," a 2003 report prepared for the Mille Lacs Band of Ojibwe in a lawsuit over the boundaries of the Mille Lacs reservation, as used in the Mille Lacs section of *This Indian Land: American Indian Activists and the Place They Made* (New York: Penguin History American Life, 2012).

17. Jensen, *Calling This Place Home*, 64–65.

18. Thomas Vennum wrote of an 1855 Indian agent's report detailing how Mille Lacs Ojibwe raised the gates on the Rum River dam to salvage their wild rice crops. Vennum, *Wild Rice and the Ojibway*, 27, also 290–96. Larsen, "A Meander Through the Big Chip."

19. Nodinens was a Mille Lacs woman who eloquently detailed the Ojibwe seasonal round to Frances Densmore.

20. Ben Gauthier was a tribal member, while his wife was non-Indian. Their Gauthier Hotel opened in 1891 as the first hotel on the reservation; it catered to lumber mill employees and was the predecessor to the resort. Surveys of Indian Industry, 282203, 28224, 282216, BIA, National Archives, Record Group 75, Great Lakes Region.

21. Lizzie Young was reportedly not in "robust health," though she still maintained a busy work life in addition to being a "good housekeeper." Surveys of Indian Industry, 282319.

For example, John Roy, aged seventy-one, "hunts, traps, and fishes," and his fifty-eight-year-old wife "Makes moccasins and reed rugs," and "they pick and can wild berries and gather wild rice. This season they made 350 pounds of maple sugar and some syrup." The government reporter included making maple sugar and wild rice as part of the wife's household labor, but probably understood the couple traveled to the wild rice and sugar bush camps together. Surveys of Indian Industry, 282210, 282215.

22. The Surveys of Indian Industry discussed approximately twenty women who were widowed, divorced, separated, or single adults at Lac du Flambeau.

23. Nesper, "Simulating Culture"; Valaskakis, "The Chippewa and the Other." Patricia Albers and William James suggest that as tourism grew in Minnesota, "the post card after 1920 lost much of its documentary role" and became "a photographic medium for tourists." Albers and James, "Images and Reality."

Itasca State Park dates from 1891, and the Douglas Lodge formally opened to visitors on June 29, 1905, when Governor John S. Johnson and his official party arrived at Itasca. The lodge was named for Wallace B. Douglas, a former Minnesota attorney general and state supreme court member. "Douglas Lodge," Minnesota Department of Natural Resources. "Indians in Minnesota Historical Pageants," *Indians At Work* (November 1, 1935). The Minnesota Historical Society has photographs of the "Chippewa Village" at Itasca State Park and the "Indian Village" at the Minnesota State Fair.

24. This Ojibwe family and others sent children to government boarding during the Great Depression. Child, *Boarding School Seasons.* See also Lomawaima, *They Called It Prairie Light;* Szasz, *Education and the American Indian.* William Watts Folwell and Melissa Meyer documented the history of land fraud and dispossession the Ojibwe faced

in Minnesota prior to the Depression. Folwell, *A History of Minnesota*, Vol. 4; Meyer, *The White Earth Tragedy*. Hilger, *Chippewa Families*.

25. Civilian Conservation Corps–Indian Division Handbook (March 1941); Series 212, Box 435, BIA, Consolidated Chippewa Agency, National Archives, Record Group 75, Kansas City.

26. Series 164, Box 362, BIA, Consolidated Chippewa Agency, National Archives, Record Group 75, Kansas City; Morrison and Galt, *Turning the Feather Around*, 47.

27. *Indians at Work* (August 15, 1933): 1–2; Series 207, Box 433, BIA, Consolidated Chippewa Agency, National Archives, Record Group 75, Kansas City; Calvin W. Gover, "The CCC Indian Division: Aid for Depressed Americans, 1933–1942," *Minnesota History* (Spring 1972): 3–13.

28. Chambliss, "Wild Rice."

29. Chambliss, "Wild Rice In Minnesota."

30. *Indians at Work* (November 15, 1934): 17.

31. The photographs appeared in *Indians at Work* (November 15, 1934): 17. The pictures stand in contrast to Densmore's 1910 photographs in which women are paired as ricing partners. Also see *Indians at Work* (November 15, 1934): 23.

32. Sugar bush "improvement projects" followed when Washington slated educational programs at the plundered White Earth Reservation "for instruction of Indians in the proper method of tapping the maple trees," complaining that Indigenous methods were "antiquated" because they did not make use of "wooden spouts" and other "modern methods." The Ojibwe were told, "If you want a steady income from your sugar bush use modern Methods. Consult your extension agent for details." *Minnesota Chippewa Bulletin* (February 23, 1940). Gathering wild fruits was also officially sanctioned when thirty boys and girls in the 4-H Club at Nett Lake were sent out to pick blueberries in the summer of 1939.

33. Simonsen, *Making Home Work*; Emmerich, "Marguerite La-Flesche Diddock." The Indian Reorganization Act of 1934, a major reform of the "Indian New Deal," remains controversial among scholars, who have at times pointed out how the federal legislation protected Indian rights, as Kenneth Philp wrote in a 1978 book, *John Collier's Crusade for Indian Reform*, while later authors have viewed the IRA more critically. For example, Biolsi, *Organizing the Lakota*.

34. Perdue, *Cherokee Women*.

35. There were other buyers in addition to LaRocque appointed by the tribe. Six Ojibwe bands in Minnesota formed the Minnesota Chippewa Tribe in 1934. The Red Lake Reservation maintained its political independence from the other Minnesota Ojibwe.

36. The Wild Rice Art and Crafts Corporation, Series 138, Box 151, BIA, National Archives, Record Group 75, Kansas City. The bulk of the records left from the cooperative is correspondence, much of it letters to individuals who purchased wild rice.

37. Little Porcupine and the Indian Maiden wear similar headbands, and the first Land O'Lakes Indian Maiden was pictured in a side pose. The Land O'Lakes corporate website details a short history of the Indian Maiden.

38. "Summary, 1939 Portage Lake Wild Rice Project," Sophia Robideau. Mrs. Shobiash was concerned about changing water levels but reported a dozen wild rice camps on Perch Lake in 1939. Series 138, Box 153, National Archives, Record Group 75, Kansas City. Vennum, *Wild Rice and the Ojibway*, 271; Coleman, "The Ojibwa and the Wild Rice Problem," 83.

39. Moyle, "The 1941 Minnesota Wild Rice Crop."

40. See, for example, "The Use of Ethnographic Data on a Modern Culture to Criticize and Reinterpret Old Accounts of Its Ancestral Culture Has Been Called Upstreaming," in Sturtevant, "Anthropology, History, and Ethnohistory."

41. Marcotty, "Iron Range Rebellion." The standards were adopted in 1973 and are based on studies conducted by Dr. John Moyle in the 1930s and 1940s which demonstrated "no large stand of rice occur in water having sulfate content greater than 10 parts per million (mg/L), and rice is generally absent from waters with more than 50 ppm." See full report, "Wild Rice Sulfate Standard Study Preliminary Analysis," www.pca.state.mn.us.

Bibliography

Interviews

Gerald Auginash, conversation with author, October 23, 2012.
Daniel Needham, interview with author, September 1987.
John D. Nichols, conversation with author, July 30, 2013.

Court Cases and Other Laws

Minnesota Statutes 1945, section 517.02
Minnesota v. Mille Lacs Band of Chippewa Indians, 526 U.S. 172 (1999).
Nelson Act, 51st Cong., 1st Sess., Ex. Doc. 247 (1889).
State of Minnesota 46th Sess., H.F. No. 540 (February 15, 1929).

Treaties

Agreement with the Red Lake Band of Chippewa Indians, 25 Stat.,
    642–46 (January 14, 1889).

Unpublished Works

Child, Brenda J. Auginash and Child Family Papers and Interviews.
    Red Lake, Minnesota.
"Chippewa Indians in Minnesota." December 26, 1998. 51st Congress,
    1st Session, House Executive Documents, no. 247—serial 2747.
Civilian Conservation Corps–Indian Division Handbook. March 1941.
Commission appointed under the Act of June 30th AD 1913. *Roll of the
    Chippewa Indians allotted within the White Earth Reservation in the
    state of Minnesota*. Minnesota Historical Society.
Frances Densmore Papers, 1867–1957. Minnesota Historical Society.
LaVoye, Lutiant. Haskell Indian Boarding School. Student File. National Archives and Records Administration.
"Lumberman's Diary, 1855." MS A-L 958. Minnesota Historical Society.

Minnesota Commission of Public Safety, 1917–19. Main Files. State Archives. Minnesota Historical Society.

Minnesota State Fisheries Department. Redby, Minnesota, 1926.

Pond Family Papers, 1833–2009. Minnesota Historical Society.

Records of the Red Lake Agency, Red Lake Band of Chippewa Indians, Red Lake, Minnesota.

———. Fred Auginash File.

———. Jeanette Jones Auginash File.

———. Interview of Peter Graves. Red Lake Tribal Archives, ca. 1950.

———. Red Lake Fisheries Association.

Records of the U.S. Bureau of Indian Affairs. National Archives and Records Administration (NARA), Record Group 75.

———. Chambliss, Charles E. "Wild Rice in Minnesota." Wild Rice Arts and Crafts Records, Series 138, Box 153.

———. *Indian Dancing*. Circular no. 1665, issued by Charles Henry Burke, Office of Indian Affairs. File 104291922–63.

———. Letters and Reports of the Office of Indian Affairs. NARA—Kansas City Branch.

———. Letters to the Minneapolis Area Office of the Bureau of Indian Affairs. Series 508793, Box 25. NARA—Kansas City Branch.

———. *Minnesota Chippewa Bulletin*. February 23, 1940. NARA—Kansas City Branch.

———. Proceedings of the General Council of the Red Lake Band of Chippewa Indians. March 1, 1929. NARA—Kansas City Branch.

———. Records of the Consolidated Chippewa Agency. NARA—Kansas City Branch.

———. Records of the Red Lake Agency. NARA—Kansas City Branch.

———. Records of the Red Lake Fisheries Association, Red Lake Agency. NARA—Kansas City Branch.

———. Report to the Interim Commission of the Minnesota State Legislature by James F. Gould, State Game and Fish Commission, Old Capitol, St. Paul, Minnesota. NARA—Kansas City Branch.

———. Robideau, Sophia. "Summary, 1939 Portage Lake Wild Rice Project." Series 138, Box 153. NARA—Kansas City Branch.

———. Surveys of Indian Industry, 1920–1922. Lac du Flambeau Agency. NARA—Great Lakes Region, Chicago.

———. The Wild Rice Art and Crafts Corporation. Series 131, Box 151. NARA—Kansas City Branch.

Thirteenth Census of the United States, 1910. Bureau of the Census, Microfilm T625, National Archives and Record Administration.

White, Bruce. "Criminalizing the Seasonal Round: Criminal and Civil Cases Limiting Ojibwe Hunting, Fishing, and Gathering, 1890–1910." Paper presented at the Annual Meeting of the American Society for Ethnohistory, 1998.

Published Works

Albers, Patricia C. "Labor and Exchange in American Indian History." In *A Companion to American Indian History,* edited by Philip J. Deloria and Neal Salisbury, 269–86. Oxford: Blackwell Publishing, 2002.

Albers, Patricia C., and Beatrice Medicine. "Some Reflections on Nearly Forty Years on the Northern Plains Powwow Circuit." In *Powwow,* edited by Clyde Ellis, Luke Eric Lassiter, and Gary H. Dunham, 26–45. Lincoln: University of Nebraska Press, 2005.

Albers, Patricia C., and William R. James. "Images and Reality: Post Cards of Minnesota's Ojibway People, 1900–80." *Minnesota History* 49.6 (Summer 1985): 229–40.

Arzigian, Constance. "Middle Woodland and Oneota Contexts for Wild Rice Exploitation in Southwestern Wisconsin." *Midcontinental Journal of Archeology* 25.2 (2000): 245–68.

Babcock, Barbara A., and Nancy J. Parezo. *Daughters of the Desert: Women Anthropologists and the Native American Southwest, 1880–1980.* Albuquerque: University of New Mexico Press, 1988.

Bauer, William J. *We Were All Like Migrant Workers Here: Work, Community and Memory on California's Round Valley Reservation.* Chapel Hill: University of North Carolina Press, 2012.

Berde, Stuart. "Wild Ricing: The Transformation of an Aboriginal Subsistence Pattern." In *Anishinabe: 6 Studies of Modern Chippewa,* edited by J. A. Paredes. Tallahassee: University Press of Florida, 1980.

Berman, Tressa. *Circle of Goods: Women, Work, and Welfare in a Reservation Community.* Albany: State University of New York Press, 2003.

Biolsi, Thomas. *Organizing the Lakota: The Political Economy of the New Deal on the Pine Ridge and Rosebud Reservations.* Tucson: University of Arizona Press, 1992.

Borrows, John. *Recovering Canada: The Resurgence of Indigenous Law.* Toronto: University of Toronto Press, 2002.

Browner, Tara. *Heartbeat of the People: Music and Dance of the Northern Pow-Wow*. Urbana and Chicago: University of Illinois Press, 2004.

Carroll, Jane Lamm. "Who Was Jane Lamont? Anglo-Dakota Daughters in Early Minnesota." *Minnesota History* 59.5 (Spring 2005): 184–96.

Catlin, George. *Letters and Notes on the Manners, Customs, and Condition of the North American Indians*. 1841. Reprint, Minneapolis: Ross and Haines, 1965.

Chambliss, Charles E. "Wild Rice." United States Department of Agriculture, Department Circular 229, August 1922.

Child, Brenda J. *Boarding School Seasons: American Indian Families, 1900–1940*. Lincoln: University of Nebraska Press, 1998.

———. *Holding Our World Together: Ojibwe Women and the Survival of Community*. New York: Penguin Books, 2012.

Clark, Jim. *Naawigiizis: The Memories of Center of the Moon, Jim Clark of Mille Lacs*. Edited by Keller Paap, Lisa LaRonge, and Heid Erdrich. Minneapolis: Birchbark Books, 2002.

Coleman, Sister Bernard. "The Ojibwa and the Wild Rice Problem." *Anthropological Quarterly* 26.3 (July 1953): 79–88.

Crosby, Alfred. *America's Forgotten Pandemic: The Influenza of 1918*. Cambridge and New York: Cambridge University Press, 2003.

Densmore, Frances. *Chippewa Customs*. 1929. Reprint, St. Paul: Minnesota Historical Society Press, 1979.

———. "Chippewa Music." Washington, DC: Bureau of American Ethnology, Bulletin 45, 1910.

———. "Chippewa Music II." Washington, DC: Bureau of American Ethnology, Bulletin 53, 1913.

———. "Uses of Plants by the Chippewa Indians." Extract from *Forty-Fourth Annual Report of the Bureau of American Ethnology*. Washington, DC: Government Printing Office, 1928.

Folwell, Williams Watts. *A History of Minnesota*. Vol. 4. St. Paul: Minnesota Historical Society, 1930.

Eastman, Charles A. *Indian Boyhood*. New York: McClure, Phillips and Co., 1902.

———. "Life and Handicrafts of the Northern Ojibwas." *The Oglala Light* (1915).

Eastman, Mary Henderson. *Dahcotah; Or, Life and Legends of the Sioux around Fort Snelling*. New York: J. Wiley, 1849.

Emmerich, Lisa E. "Marguerite LaFlesche Diddock: Office of Indian Affairs Field Matron." *Great Plains Quarterly* 13 (Summer 1993): 162–71.

Hagg, Harold T. "Logging Line: A History of the Minneapolis, Red Lake and Manitoba." *Minnesota History* 43.4 (Winter 1972): 123–35.

Hickerson, Harold. *The Chippewa and Their Neighbors: A Study in Ethnohistory.* New York: Holt, Rinehart and Winston, 1970.

Hilger, M. Inez. *Chippewa Families: A Social Study of White Earth Reservation.* 1938. Reprint, St. Paul: Minnesota Historical Society Press, 1998.

Hosmer, Brian C. *American Indians in the Marketplace: Persistence and Innovation among the Menominees and Metlakatlans, 1870–1920.* Lawrence: University of Kansas Press, 1999.

Hosmer, Brian C., Alexandra Harmon, and Colleen O'Neill. "Interwoven Economic Histories: American Indians in a Capitalist America." *Journal of American History* 98.3 (2011): 698–722.

Hoxie, Frederick. *The Final Promise: The Campaign to Assimilate the Indians, 1880–1920.* Lincoln: University of Nebraska Press, 1984.

———. *This Indian Country: American Indian Activists and the Place They Made.* New York: Penguin Group, 2012.

Hyman, Colette A. *Dakota Women's Work: Creativity, Culture, and Exile.* St. Paul: Minnesota Historical Society Press, 2012.

Jenks, Albert E. "The Wild Rice Gatherers of the Upper Lakes: A Study in American Primitive Economics." *Nineteenth Annual Report of the Bureau of American Ethnology, 1897–98,* 1013–137. Washington, DC: Government Printing Office, 1900.

Jensen, Joan M. *Calling This Place Home: Women on the Wisconsin Frontier, 1850–1925.* St. Paul: Minnesota Historical Society Press, 2006.

Joe, Jennie R., and Robert S. Young, eds. *Diabetes as a Disease of Civilization: The Impact of Culture Change on Indigenous Peoples.* Berlin: Walter de Gruyter & Co., 1983.

Kegg, Maude. *Portage Lake: Memories of an Ojibwe Childhood.* Edited by John D. Nichols. Edmonton: University of Alberta Press, 1991.

Kelly, Lawrence C. *The Assault on Assimilation: John Collier and the Origins of Indian Policy Reform.* Albuquerque: University of New Mexico Press, 1983.

La Farge, Oliver. *Laughing Boy: A Navajo Love Story.* 1929. Reprint, Boston: Mariner Books, 2004.

Larsen, Ray. "A Meander Through the Big Chip." *Wisconsin Department of Natural Resources Magazine* (October/November 1997).

LaVoye, Lutiant. Miscellaneous Letters. "The Deadly Virus: The Influenza Epidemic of 1918." *Regional History from the National Archives.* http://www.archives.gov/exhibits/influenza-epidemic/.

Lieberman, Shari. "A Review of the Effectiveness of *Cimicifuga racemosa* (Black Cohosh) for the Symptoms of Menopause." *Journal of Women's Health* 7.5 (June 1998): 525–29.

Liebling, Phyllis L., and Jerome Liebling. "A Visit to Red Lake." *The Massachusetts Review* 2.1 (Autumn 1960): 139–52.

Littlefield, Alice, and March C. Knack, eds. *Native Americans and Wage Labor: Ethnohistorical Perspectives.* Norman: University of Oklahoma Press, 1996.

Lomawaima, K. Tsianina. *They Called It Prairie Light: The Story of Chilocco Indian School.* Lincoln: University of Nebraska Press, 1995.

Marcotty Josephine. "Iron Range Rebellion Halted Wild Rice Initiative." *Minneapolis Star Tribune,* April 7, 2014.

McClurken James M., Charles E. Cleland, Thomas Lund, John D. Nichols, Helen Tanner, and Bruce White. *Fish in the Lakes, Wild Rice, and Game in Abundance: Testimony on Behalf of Mille Lacs Ojibwe Hunting and Fishing Rights.* East Lansing: Michigan State University Press, 2000.

McMillen, Christian W. *Making Indian Law: The Hualapai Land Case and the Birth of Ethnohistory.* New Haven: Yale University Press, 2007.

Meyer, Melissa. *The White Earth Tragedy: Ethnicity and Dispossession at a Minnesota Anishinaabe Reservation, 1889–1920.* Lincoln: University of Nebraska Press, 1994.

Minnesota Pollution Control Agency. "Wild Rice Sulfate Standard Study Preliminary Analysis." March 2014. http://www.pca.state.mn.us/index.php/view-document.html?gid=20743.

Mittleholtz, Erwin F. "Historical Review of the Red Lake Indian Reservation, Centennial Souvenir Commemorating a Century of Progress, 1858–1958." Published by the General Council of the Red Lake Band of Chippewa Indians and the Beltrami County Historical Society, August 1957.

Morrison, George, and Margot Fotunato Galt. *Turning The Feather Around: My Life in Art.* St. Paul: Minnesota Historical Society Press, 1998.

Moyle, John B. "The 1941 Minnesota Wild Rice Crop." St. Paul: Bureau of Fisheries Research Division of Game and Fish, State of Minnesota, 39.

Neihardt, John C. *Black Elk Speaks: Being the Life Story of a Holy Man of the Oglala Sioux.* 1932. Reprint, Lincoln: University of Nebraska Press, 1988.

Nesper, Larry. "Simulating Culture: Being Indian for Tourists in Lac du Flambeau's Wa-Swa-Gon Indian Bowl." *Ethnohistory* 50.3 (Summer 2003): 447–72.

Nichols, John D., and Earl Nyholm. *A Concise Dictionary of Minnesota Ojibwe.* Minneapolis: University of Minnesota Press, 1995.

O'Neill, Colleen. *Working the Navajo Way: Labor and Culture in the Twentieth Century.* Lawrence: University Press of Kansas, 2005.

Osburn, Katherine M. B. *Southern Ute Women: Autonomy and Assimilation on the Reservation, 1887–1934.* Lincoln: University of Nebraska Press, 2009.

Ostler, Jeffrey. *The Plains Sioux and U.S. Colonialism from Lewis and Clark to Wounded Knee.* New York: Cambridge University Press, 2004.

Pascoe, Peggy. *What Comes Naturally: Miscegenation Law and the Making of Race in America.* New York: Oxford University Press, 2010.

Peers, Laura. *The Ojibwa of Western Canada: 1780–1870.* St. Paul: Minnesota Historical Society Press, 1994.

Perdue, Theda. *Cherokee Women: Gender and Culture Change, 1700–1835.* Lincoln: University of Nebraska Press, 1998.

Philp, Kenneth. *John Collier's Crusade for Indian Reform, 1920–1954.* Tucson: University of Arizona Press, 1977.

Raibmon, Paige. *Authentic Indians: Episodes of Encounter from the Late-Nineteenth-Century Northwest Coast.* Durham and London: Duke University Press, 2005.

Red Lake Band of Anishinaabe, "Constitution of the Red Lake Band of Anishinaabe (1918)." In *Documents of Native American Political Development: 1500s to 1933,* edited by David E. Wilkins, 408–9. New York: Oxford University Press, 2009.

Ritzenthaler, Robert E., and Pat Ritzenthaler. *The Woodland Indians of the Western Great Lakes.* Garden City, NY: Natural History Press, 1970.

Rogers, John. *Red World and White: Memories of a Chippewa Boyhood.* 1957. Reprint, Norman: University of Oklahoma Press, 1996.

Sandefur, Gary D., Ronald R. Rindfuss, and Barney Cohen. *Changing Numbers, Changing Needs: American Indian Demography and Public Health.* Washington, DC: National Academies Press, 1996.

Schoolcraft, Henry R. *Summary Narrative of an Exploratory Expedition to the Sources of the Mississippi River, in 1820.* Philadelphia: Lippincott, Grambo, and Co., 1855.

Selvog, S. A. "State Fisheries Activities During 1925." Official Bulletin of the Minnesota Game and Fish Department, *Fins, Feathers, and Fur* 136 (December 1925): 53–62.

Shoemaker, Nancy. *Negotiators of Change: Historical Perspectives on Native American Women.* New York: Routledge, 1995.

Simonsen, Jane E. *Making Home Work: Domesticity and Native American Assimilation in the American West, 1860–1919.* Chapel Hill: University of North Carolina Press, 2006.

Smith, Linda Tuhiwai. *Decolonizing Methodologies: Research and Indigenous Peoples.* 2nd ed. London: Zed Books, Ltd., 2012.

Stanchfield, Daniel. "History of Lumbering in Minnesota." *Collections of the Minnesota Historical Society* 9 (1901).

Sturtevant, William C. "Anthropology, History, and Ethnohistory." *Ethnohistory* 13 (Winter/Spring 1966): 1–51.

Szasz, Margaret Connell. *Education and the American Indian: The Road to Self-Determination Since 1928.* 3rd ed. Albuquerque: University of New Mexico Press, 1999.

Thiel, Mark. "Origins of the Jingle Dress Dance." *Whispering Wind* 36.5 (Issue 255): 14–18.

Thwaites, Rueben G., ed. "Radisson and Groseilliers in Wisconsin." *Collections of the State Historical Society of Wisconsin* 11 (1888).

Treuer, Anton, ed. *Living Our Language: Ojibwe Tales and Oral Histories.* St. Paul: Minnesota Historical Society Press, 2001.

Troutman, John W. *Indian Blues: American Indians and the Politics of Music, 1879–1934.* Norman: University of Oklahoma Press, 2012.

United States, Office of Indian Affairs. *Indians At Work.* Washington, DC: Bureau of Indian Affairs, 1933–45.

Valaskakis, Gail Guthrie. "The Chippewa and the Other: Living the Heritage of Lac du Flambeau." *Cultural Studies* 2.3 (1988): 267–93.

Vennum, Thomas, Jr. *The Ojibwa Dance Drum: Its History and Construction.* Washington, DC: Smithsonian Institution Press, 1982.

———. "The Ojibway Begging Dance." In *Music and Context: Essays for John M. Ward*, edited by Anne D. Shapiro, 54–78. Cambridge: Department of Music, Harvard University, 1985.

———. *Wild Rice and the Ojibway People*. St. Paul: Minnesota Historical Society Press, 1988.

Vizenor, Gerald, and Jill Doerfler, eds. *The White Earth Nation: Ratification of a Native Democratic Constitution*. Lincoln: University of Nebraska Press, 2012.

Warren, William W. *History of the Ojibway People*. 1885. Reprint, St. Paul: Minnesota Historical Society Press, 1984.

White, Bruce. *We Are at Home: Pictures of the Ojibwe People*. St. Paul: Minnesota Historical Society Press, 2007.

Wilkins, David E., ed. *Documents of Native American Political Development: 1500s to 1933*. New York: Oxford University Press, 2009.

Witgen, Michael. *An Infinity of Nations: How the Native New World Shaped Early North America*. Philadelphia: University of Pennsylvania Press, 2012.

Woolworth, Nancy L. "Miss Densmore Meets the Ojibwe: Frances Densmore's Ethnomusicology Studies Among the Grand Portage Ojibwe in 1905." *Minnesota Archeologist* 38.3 (August 1979): 106–28.

Young, T. Kue. "Recent Health Trends in the Native American Population." In *Changing Numbers, Changing Needs: American Indian Demography and Public Health*, edited by Gary Sandefur, Ronald R. Rindfuss, and Barney Cohen, 53–76. Washington, DC: The National Academies Press, 1996.

Index

Abbreviations "FA" and "JA" stand for Fred Auginash and Jeanette Jones Auginash, respectively. Ojibwe words and names are shown in italics. Page numbers in italics indicate photographs.

Photo Credits

Pages 19, 20, 29, 67, 70, 76, 193
   Family photos
Page 45
   Fred Auginash File, Records of the Red Lake Agency, Redlake, MN
Pages 86, 90, 99, 102, 109, 147, 152, 178
   Record Group 75, Records of the Bureau of Indian Affairs,
   1793–1999; Red Lake Agency: Photographs, 1910–65, National
   Archives and Records Administration
Pages 97, 107 (photo by Jerome Liebling), 133, 143, 165, 168, 169, 184
(photo by Monroe Killy), 186 (photo by Monroe Killy), 188, 191
   Minnesota Historical Society collections
Pages 111 (photo by Inez Hilger), 127, 137
   Marquette University collections
Page 135
   Courtesy Pat Albers

CPSIA information can be obtained
at www.ICGtesting.com
Printed in the USA
JSHW021215150321
12536JS00001B/102